Predestination! What far depths conceal
  From feeble sight, unable to detect
  The First Cause whole, thy root of woe and weal!

And, Mortals, keep your judgement straitly checked,
  For here we see God face to face, and still
  We know not all the roll of his elect;

Yet sweet to us appears our lack of skill,
  Since this good doth our good the more refine,
  That what God willeth, that we also will.

    —Dante, *The Divine Comedy*, 3, 20, 130–38

ELECTION and PREDESTINATION

by
Paul K. Jewett

with a foreword by Vernon Grounds

WILLIAM B. EERDMANS PUBLISHING COMPANY
THE PATERNOSTER PRESS

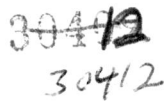

Copyright © 1985 by Wm. B. Eerdmans Publishing Company
All rights reserved
Printed in the United States of America
for
William B. Eerdmans Publishing Company
255 Jefferson Ave. S.E., Grand Rapids, Mich. 49503
and
The Paternoster Press Ltd.
3 Mount Radford Crescent, Exeter, Devon, UK EX2 4JW

Library of Congress Cataloging-in-Publication Data:

Jewett, Paul King.
  Election and predestination.
  Includes index.
  1. Election (Theology) I. Title.
BT810.2.J48 1985   234   85-20725

ISBN 0-8028-0090-4 (pbk.)

British Library Cataloguing in Publication Data:

Jewett, Paul K.
  Election and predestination.
  1. Election (Theology)
  I. Title
  234'.9   BT810.2

ISBN 0-85364-438-1

Contents

Foreword	vii
Preface	x
Introduction	1

1 A Historical Overview — 5
   The Ancient Church — 5
   The Medieval Church — 7
   From the Reformation to the Present — 10
   Addendum: The Place of the Doctrine in Systematics — 22

2 The Biblical Data Summarized — 24

3 Election and the People of God — 30
   The Church the Heir of Israel's Election — 31
   What of the Jewish People? — 34
      1. The Traditional Answer — 34
      2. Their Election Affirmed — 38
      3. Israel's Future and the Christian Vision — 39
   Addendum: A Parenthetical Remark on Dispensationalism — 45

4 Election and the Individual — 47
   A Summary of Barth's View — 48
   Election and Jesus Christ — 54
   Addendum: Concerning Assurance and the Syllogismus Practicus — 57

Efforts at Understanding	61
1. Election and Foreknowledge	67
Addendum: Election and Free Will	73
2. Election and Predestination	77
3. The Divine Will as Antecedent and Consequent	97
First Addendum: A Comment on Amyrauldism	101
Second Addendum: Universal Language and the Property of Ambiguity	102
Some Reflections on the Mystery of Grace	106
1. The Dynamic Relation of Eternity to Time	109
2. The Universal in the Particular	115
First Addendum: Election and the Question of Numbers	121
Second Addendum: Election and Preaching	128
Concerning Wonder and Worship	133
Index of Names and Subjects	141
Index of Scripture References	144

Foreword

To commend a book by a friend is a privilege—provided the commendation is elicited not by a relationship rooted in *auld lang syne* but solely by the merit of the author's scholarship and insight. Such happily is the case with Paul Jewett's *Election and Predestination*. It is a privilege indeed to commend this splendid specimen of theological craftsmanship.

My friendship with Dr. Jewett, stretching back over long years, has been life-enriching. I have come to know him as a deeply devout brother, an erudite teacher, a Christian with a passionate concern for truth and justice. I therefore read anything he writes with a positive bias, confident that it will be not only a solid piece of careful research and deep reflection but an exercise in critical intelligence on the highest level as well. It will also be a praiseworthy example of irenic fairness. So I anticipated that dealing with even the volatile issues of election and predestination, which through the centuries have aroused fiercest controversy, my friend would once again confirm my positive prejudice. He did precisely that.

In my opinion, Dr. Jewett has given to the whole church a study from which adherents of all views on these high and difficult issues will greatly profit. In a succinct historical overview he presents a crystal-clear analysis of the strengths and weaknesses of the arguments employed by the major proponents and antagonists of rival positions in this never-ending debate. I for one found illuminating his incisive interaction with Calvin, Amyrauldus, and Barth, for example. (Dr. Jewett rightly and critically focuses attention on Barth's reinterpretation of election which has exerted such a powerful influence.) I also found illuminating, as every reader will, his discussion of such weighty subjects as supralapsarianism, infralapsarianism, the choice and rejection of Israel (this especially), the impingement of God's sovereign foreknowledge on human freedom, and the ambiguity of language.

As an unequivocal evangelical, my friend recognizes that in the end exegetical constraints must be decisive. Yet he makes us freshly aware that even hermeneutically there has been no commanding consensus regarding the revelational data on these components of God's redemptive process.

Repeatedly Dr. Jewett reminds us that tensions arise as we probe this area of theology, to say nothing of other areas — tensions that logic is incapable of eliminating. Thus, after thoroughly considering the problem of reprobation, he admits that it "remains unresolved and, it would appear, unresolvable." Pointing out consequently that mystery merges into paradox, he raises that mind-boggling question which has perplexed generations of believers: "If the Holy One revealed in Scripture is love, how can he be the God who predestines his creatures to sin in order that he might condemn them?" In short, rather than denying that biblical doctrine embraces antinomies, he affirms their presence. For example, on the one hand Scripture teaches that every human action falls within the will of God, yet on the other hand it uniformly contends that man's sin is against the will of God. Concisely summarizing the ultimate imponderability of divine truth, Dr. Jewett expresses my own belief far better than I am able to do:

> To *confess* such a truth is not to *explain* it. Mystery confronts us on every side. Formal logic would suggest that where we have paradox, we have a screw loose in our argument. But there is a difference between those paradoxes that result from fallacious argument and paradoxes that mark the limits of human thought. All rational thinkers have been compelled to recognize the seeming finality of paradox in this latter sense, the existence of the so-called *insolubilia*.

Thus a superlative value of Dr. Jewett's book from my perspective is his emphasis on the inescapability of paradox. Since I am personally and profoundly persuaded that the logic of faith necessitates the postulation of paradox, I am grateful to have my convictions so ably articulated.

FOREWORD

I applaud the integrity of my Calvinistic friend who declines the role of an uncommitted dialectician toying with ambiguous concepts. Instead of that, in the very spirit of "wonder and worship" that he espouses, Dr. Jewett joins with Paul in an adoring submission of heart *and* mind. "O the depth of the riches of the wisdom and knowledge of God! Who has known the mind of the Lord? Or who has been his counselor? Who has ever given to God, that God should repay him? For from him and through him and to him are all things. To him be the glory forever! Amen."

VERNON GROUNDS

Preface

When one teaches theology to a large number of students in a multidenominational setting, as it has been my privilege to do, one knows that the doctrine of election will surely evoke questions. But it is not just the students who ask questions about the subject. In fact, the questions students ask simply echo those the theologians have asked and continue to ask themselves. The common assumption that the classroom is the place where there are students who have questions and professors who have answers is an egregious oversimplification, especially when it comes to classes in theology. I say this because theology is not concerned with truths accessible to reason alone, nor with truths based on the "assured results" of empirical observation. While theologians ought not to affirm something to be true for faith that is contrary to reason or that denies sense observation, they should (and do) affirm truths based on revelation and accepted by faith. Hence the teacher of theology is not one who simply "has the answers" but rather one who so expounds and shares possible answers that students are confronted with the need to decide for themselves and thus to find the answers that enable each one to say, "This I believe and this is why I believe it."

In this process, the teacher leads the way, pointing the students to the Scriptures and to the answers that have commended themselves to those Christians who have read and pondered the Scriptures before them. In doing this, the teacher cannot—so far as my experience goes—avoid making decisions too. The decisions I have made, when it comes to the doctrine of election, obviously put me on the Augustinian and Reformed side of the theological universe. Why I have made the decisions that I have, how I draw out their implications, and what conclusions I have reached will be evident as the argument unfolds. Whatever decisions my readers may come to as they follow the argument, I can only hope that what I have written will be of help to them in making these decisions their own.

To that end I have taken time to write this little book on a subject on which first my teachers and then my students have made me think a great deal. For that and for them I am most grateful. For the benefit of those who have never sat in the classroom with me and are therefore unfamiliar with the approach I take, the following summary of the argument may prove helpful.

I begin with a historical overview, not only to illustrate the persistence and complexity of the debate but also to give a sense of bearing to those evaluating the issues. I turn next to the biblical data, which I review in a way that reflects the tension found throughout Scripture between God's choice of the sinner and the sinner's choice of God. Having set up the problem, I begin my own quest for an answer with a consideration of corporate election. In this section I give special attention to Israel and to the question of how those of God's chosen people who are Jews are related to the church, the heir of Israel's election and covenant. I turn next to the question of election and the individual, a section in which I pause to give special attention to Barth's unique attempt to resolve the issue in terms of the election (and rejection) of Jesus Christ. I agree with Barth that Christ, as the elect, is the mirror of our own election, but I do not embrace the universalism implied in his doctrine.

Turning to a more traditional view of election, especially as that view has been defended in the theology coming out of Geneva, I probe the issue of methodology. While I cannot accept the Eastern Orthodox and Arminian view that understands the divine choice in terms of the human choice—I find the exegetical problems with such a position insuperable—neither can I say that the efforts of Augustine and his followers to understand the human choice in terms of the divine choice are altogether convincing. The supralapsarian view, which is logically satisfying, is in my judgment morally intolerable, while the infralapsarian view, for all the amelioration it provides, is logically inadequate.

I conclude the discussion, therefore, by highlighting the element of mystery in the doctrine of grace and the response of gratitude and worship that such mystery evokes. In doing so, as the occasion demands, I reflect on the dynamic relationship of eternity to time, the way in which Scripture relates the universal to the particular, the question of numbers—of "thinking small," which is so hard for Americans—and the relation of election to preaching, which is the primary task of the church and the forerunner of all theology.

A special word of thanks is due to Fuller Seminary for affording me the opportunity to teach and the time to write about theology—particularly about such a difficult and important subject as election—and to teaching assistants, former students, and others who have assisted me in typing and editing the manuscript for publication.

PAUL K. JEWETT
Pasadena, California
1985

Note on Abbreviations: The following two works are cited parenthetically in the text, using the abbreviations here given:

CD = Barth, Karl. *Church Dogmatics*. 5 vols. Edited by Geoffrey W. Bromiley and Thomas F. Torrance. Translated by Geoffrey W. Bromiley et al. Edinburgh: T. & T. Clark, 1955–77.

Inst. = Calvin, John. *Institutes of the Christian Religion*. 2 vols. Edited by John T. McNeill. Translated by Ford Lewis Battles. Library of Christian Classics, vols. 20–21. Philadelphia: Westminster Press, 1960.

Unless otherwise indicated, all Scripture quotations in the publication are from the Revised Standard Version of the Bible, copyrighted 1946, 1952 © 1971, 1973 by the Division of Christian Education of the National Council of Churches of Christ in the U.S.A., and used by permission.

Introduction

There are two things about the doctrine of election that cannot be gainsaid: it is important, and it is controversial. Its importance can be measured by such criteria as (1) the place allotted to the theme in Scripture—the subject is so pervasive it can hardly be avoided; (2) the attention given the question by all the major confessions and theologians; and (3) the fact that confession of the doctrine is a distinguishing characteristic of a leading branch of the Christian family called Reformed and Presbyterian.

As for the controversial character of the doctrine, while it is true that controversy is essential to doctrinal development, there is nevertheless something uncommonly persistent about the argument over election. Here is an argument that has endured so long and engendered so much feeling that the very terms *predestination, foreordination*, and *election* have become symbols of divisiveness. Probably no other doctrine is so frequently dismissed as "too controversial." And the controversy is not only enduring but also perplexing. As originally debated by Pelagius and Augustine, it was obviously productive. To this controversy we owe the doctrine of grace, so basic to the Christian vision. But in the ensuing centuries the argument has often seemed counterproductive.[1] Furthermore, the controversy

---

1. "Augustine's predestination was safe with him," observes Charles Williams, "comprehensible in Calvin, tiresome in the English Puritans, and quite horrible in the Scottish presbyteries" (*The Descent of the Dove: A Short History of the Holy Spirit in the Church* [1939; Grand Rapids: William B. Eerdmans, 1980], p. 191).

has been extended by implication to many another doctrine, including those of God, humankind, sin, and salvation. Its sheer scope and complexity is enough to dismay even the patient student. Is God an arbitrary tyrant? Is human freedom an illusion? Is the death of Christ for nought in those who are not elect? Is the call to the sinner sincere in every instance?

Finally, even those theologians who subscribe to the doctrine cannot agree on just what the problem is, let alone how it is to be resolved. Is it that some have tried to pry between the pages of destiny when they should have kept silent before the adorable mystery of the divine counsel? Or is an appeal to a mysterious counsel, a "secret decree," a denial of the central truth that God in Christ is not the hidden God but the revealed God, the God who has made known his electing will, his Yes toward us, in love and compassion? Or again, is the problem that some have conceived the electing will of God *causally*, so that the "pre" of *predestination* becomes the initial segment on the time line that reduces everything that follows to meaninglessness? Or yet again, does the problem consist in the fact that many have misunderstood the *object* of predestination, that when they should have thought of the object of election as Christ, the chosen Servant of the Lord, they have instead thought of a fixed number of individuals, the "roll of the elect," and have thus been driven to the inescapable inference that there is also a fixed number of nonelect for whom there is no hope—that there is a Book of Death along with a Book of Life?

Even as theologians have not been able to agree on the problem, so they have not been able to agree on the solution—or indeed even on the proper procedure to follow in seeking a solution. On the one hand, there are those who want to regard the whole matter *sub specie temporis* (i.e., from the perspective of time). Election should always be related not to a past eternity but to the saving events of holy history. Those given to such an approach construe election as the *ex post facto* explanation of why some believe and some do not. Only after the doctrines of repentance, faith, and renewal have been interpreted historically—that is, from the perspective of *Heilsgeschichte*—should we be concerned with the doctrine of an eternal election. Some go so far as to say that only as we begin with the choice of the creature (faith) rather than with the eternal choice of the Creator (election) can we escape the labyrinthine questions posed by the lapsarian controversy, the profound abyss of speculation into which the dogmaticians fell in the age of scholastic Calvinism.[2]

On the other hand there are those who regard the doctrine of election *sub specie aeternitatis* (i.e., from the perspective of eternity). Such a view is obviously more tenable for one who approaches Scripture as the Reformers did, but it is not without its problems. Given such a view, election is not only a matter of salvation by grace (Augustine), but more basically it is the unfolding of the eternal purpose of God. Those who take this position must exercise care lest they lose the doctrine of the election of grace in a general doctrine of predestination that becomes hardly distinguishable from Stoic fatalism. Furthermore, while it is tempting to the systematician to try to deduce the doctrine of salvation from the doctrine of God, we must remember that this cannot be done. It was not a matter of necessity that God should have created us, much less redeemed us. Salvation is not the implication of God's nature but the free gift of his grace.

Yet for all these differences of opinion concerning the nature of the problem and how to proceed toward its resolution, it is not too much to say that every theologian of the first rank from Augustine to Barth has affirmed the doctrine of election as basic to the Christian faith. Nor is this consensus merely formal. These master theologians have also agreed in a material way on the essential content of the doctrine.[3] They all contend that God's election is a righteous and holy decision that he makes according to his own good

---

2. In modern times H. H. Rowley reflects this historical perspective in the way in which he virtually identifies the "election" of Israel with the "covenant" of Israel. "Their divine election and covenant is [sic] never merely automatic. It must be renewed by each generation of those that inherit it" (*The Biblical Doctrine of Election* [London: Lutterworth, 1950], pp. 16, 34). Hence, Rowley can announce straight off that he will not deal with predestination to salvation and condemnation, since "this is an entirely different question from the one before us"—namely, the biblical doctrine of election (p. 16). Such an obvious confusion of the *ratio essendi* with the *ratio cognoscendi* simply reduces the term *election* to its historical result. A more correct statement of the case, in my judgment, is (in the words of G. Ernest Wright) that Israel's election is *unto* covenant. Election and covenant, in other words, are distinct; they do not take a singular verb.

3. The exception is Schleiermacher, whose redefinition of the Christian faith as a whole obviously eliminates any material agreement with his predecessors on the meaning of election. See pp. 17−19 herein.

pleasure to redeem the objects of his electing love. Essential as is the decision on the sinner's part to accept the salvation offered in the gospel, this human decision is ultimately grounded in the divine decision. Election means that God's grace is not evoked by any claim or merit in the creature but comes to the creature as a miracle the ground of which is the personal freedom and sovereign good pleasure of God, our Maker and Redeemer. All these theologians would also agree that inasmuch as election is God's free choice, not determined by his foresight of the sinner's choice, we can never probe the mystery of the divine counsel or give a final reason for it. God's will is its own warrant, its own final reason. Yet our confession that we are saved by the electing grace of God is not a *sacrificium intellectus*; it is rather a confession to which we are brought as we are taught by his Spirit. To confess that we are elect is to contemplate our salvation with humility and adoration and to acknowledge that it is a gratuitous act of divine mercy.

Having said this much by way of introduction, our first major task will be the exposition of the doctrine. But before we turn to that task, a brief historical overview is in order. Such an overview will, I hope, acquaint readers not only with what Christians in other ages have thought and said but also enable them to relate my exposition of the doctrine to that ongoing discussion. This historical review will conclude with a brief section on the place of the doctrine in the structure of dogmatics, a question ever present to the systematician whose concern is not only the exposition of the doctrines of the faith but also their relationship to one another.

1
A Historical Overview

THE ANCIENT CHURCH

As has often been observed, the first true predestinarian was Augustine. To be sure, various Fathers of the church before him touched upon the subject,[1] but as a whole they opposed the concept of predestination that he came to espouse. From the time of Justin, the Greek theologians of the East responded to widespread Stoic determinism and popular astral fatalism by stressing the freedom of the human will in a way that made it impossible for them to espouse a doctrine of divine foreordination along Augustinian lines even when interpreting Paul. To them the natural ability of sinners to turn from their sin in response to the preaching mission of the church was simply assumed as beyond question. This assumption explains why the views of the British monk Pelagius were, in a somewhat modified form, widely accepted throughout the ancient Eastern church. Like the Eastern church in general, Pelagius could not pray the prayer of Augustine: "Give what thou commandest and command what thou wilt" (*Conf.*, 1.10.C.29). To him it was self-evident that a commandment on God's part presupposed the ability to obey on the creature's part.

Augustine's experience of sin and grace and his understanding of Paul compelled him to come to another conclusion. Not only

---

1. Especially Athanasius; see *Orationes contra Arianos* 2, 77ff. in *Patrologia Graeca*, ed. J. P. Migne, 162 vols. (Turnhout: Brepols, 1857–66), 26: 306ff.

ELECTION AND PREDESTINATION

Christ's objective work of salvation but the human response to that work as well were of God.[2] In other words, salvation is wholly of grace. Hence the difference between those who accept and those who reject the gospel is not ultimately a matter of the human will but of the divine will. Behind the human decision in time is a divine decision made from eternity. God's purpose is realized in both those who believe and those who reject the gospel: the hardened (reprobate) receive his wrath, and the saved (elect) receive his mercy. This double predestination, gracious in those who are saved from their sins and just in those who are condemned for their sins, is ultimately a mystery that only presumption would seek to explain, while faith would adore.[3] God's judgments are unsearchable and his ways past finding out (Rom. 11:33). The City of God (the church) is the whole number of the elect who have been, are, and shall be saved. And because the church is made up of individuals, the number of the elect, according to Augustine, is a specific and particular number. This number, unknown to us, is known to God, for known to God are all his works from before the foundation of the world (Acts 15:18).

Augustine clearly won the day against Pelagius, whose teachings were condemned; but his doctrine of predestination, especially as it involved *double* predestination—that is, the predestination of the reprobate as well as the elect[4]—was largely ignored in the Eastern church. Even in the Western church, double predestination was never accepted by many who were otherwise Augustine's disciples.

---

2. Pelagius wrote his commentary on the Pauline epistles in A.D. 409. The position he represents, especially as worked out by his leading disciple Celestius, may be called "*human* monergism," since it assumes that the power of the human will is decisive in the experience of salvation. It was actually in response to this human monergism that Augustine championed a divine monergism, although his position is more often contrasted with the synergism of the semi-Pelagians, which seeks to coordinate the human will and divine grace in some form of mutual cooperation.

3. In Protestant vocabulary, the term *predestination* is often used in a general sense to express the thought that all that happens is predetermined by God and occurs according to his will. Some speak of predestination in this sense as "general predestination" in distinction to "specific" or "soteric" or "double predestination" (*gemina predestinatio*), so called because it involves predestination to salvation (election) or condemnation (reprobation); see Heppe, *Reformed Dogmatics* (London: Allen and Unwin, 1950), pp. 151, 154.

4. Augustine does not speak of predestination to sin, but of predestination to perdition as the punishment of sin.

In the ensuing controversy many efforts were made to establish a position between that of Augustine and Pelagius. These efforts addressed themselves to a persistent problem known as the "paradox of grace"—namely, the sovereignty of the divine choice and the responsibility of the human choice. At the Synod of Orange (A.D. 529) a moderate Augustinianism prevailed. Based largely on the writings of Prosper of Aquitaine and Caesarius of Arles, this semi-Augustinianism (synergism) did not resolve the paradox, but it did espouse a doctrine that was nearer the monergism of Augustine than the synergism of Pelagius.

This milder predestinarianism became the official teaching of the Latin church. This teaching affirms God's eternal predestination to salvation (election), but it does not go on to affirm predestination to perdition (reprobation). Indeed, it suggests that the reprobate are condemned to eternal death not because of God's decree but because their resistance to the grace of God proves, in the end, to be incorrigible. Furthermore, in the case of the elect, though their faith is the gift of grace (*gratia praeveniens*), this grace is not so irresistible (*gratia irresistibilus*) as to violate the freedom of the creature who persists in his sin.

THE MEDIEVAL CHURCH

The decision of Orange did not put an end to the controversy. In the West the original doctrine of Augustine continued to have its adherents (e.g., Bede, Alcuin, Isidore of Seville) and in the ninth century underwent something of a revival fired by the ardor of the Benedictine monk Gottschalk, an avid student of Augustine's writings. As the champion of double predestination, Gottschalk was opposed by Rabanus Maurus, who insisted that while punishment is ordained for sinners in general, no sinner in particular is ordained to punishment.[5] The storm of controversy that gathered around

---

5. Gottschalk faced opposition of another order from Hincmar, the intolerant archbishop of Rheims, who had him scourged "most atrociously" and incarcerated for twenty years, refusing him Communion during his last illness and then refusing him burial in consecrated ground. The "miserable monk" died unshaken in his faith (A.D. 868 or 869), condemned as an obstinate heretic by his enemies but revered by later Jansenists and Calvinists as a martyr to the doctrine of free grace. See Philip Schaff, *History of the Christian Church*, 8 vols. (New York: Scribners, 1910), 4: 525ff.

Gottschalk and his followers contributed little to the resolution of the problem. It was argued by many of semi-Pelagian persuasion that God's election and reprobation are based on his foreknowledge of who will accept (or reject) the gospel. Those on the other side protested that to ground election in foreseen faith is to subvert the doctrine of *sola gratia* by making salvation a matter of human merit. As for human freedom, the semi-Augustinians/Pelagians argued that though the fallen descendants of Adam have lost the original freedom with which the head of the race was created, they nevertheless retain sufficient freedom and ability to accept (or reject) the grace offered in Christ. The followers of Augustine agreed that sinners are indeed free from all fatalistic necessity and coercion, but, since God is omnipotent and unchangeable, what he has predetermined according to his own counsel and will cannot be nullified by the will of the sinful creature.

Though all parties tended to accept this immutability of the divine will and purpose, some insisted that God's foreknowledge could be distinguished in its scope from his predestination; God infallibly foreknows both whom he has predestined to salvation (the elect) and whom he has not so predestined (the reprobate). In other words, his foreknowledge is double, but his predestination (purpose) is single. Some of the Augustinians themselves preferred to speak of a single rather than a double predestination, but they sought to embrace both the gift of God's grace and the exercise of his justice in this single predestination. Among those who argued in this fashion, some spoke of the predestination of the reprobate in terms of a predestination *of* punishment, but not *to* punishment. Those who followed Gottschalk tended to view this distinction as an evasion. They reasoned that while it is true that God has predestined punishment to sinners for their sins, it is also true that he has predestined sinners to the punishment their sin deserves.

In the midst of this ofttimes acrimonious debate, scriptures on both sides were easily quoted but not so easily harmonized. How could it be that the God who "has mercy on whom he will and hardens whom he will" (Rom. 9:18) is also the God who is not willing "that any should perish but that all should come to repentance" (2 Pet. 3:9)? If he wills that all should repent, how is it that he hardens some?

In the high Middle Ages, theologians were more concerned

with general system making than with breaking new ground in specific areas. Yet precisely because of this overriding interest in systematic theology, there were certain questions they could not possibly avoid. Of these, none was more obvious than the question of predestination and free will. The efforts at resolution, therefore, continued unabated. Anselm, for example, made much of the fact—which had already been noted in the prior course of the controversy—that, strictly speaking, God does not predestine anything, since to him all things are present at one and the same time: for God there is no past or future but only an eternal present. Hence, freedom of human choice is compatible not only with the divine foreknowledge but also with predestination. While many continued to lay the stress on foreknowledge as the key to understanding— God predestines what he foresees will happen—Bonaventura and his followers grounded the certainty of predestination not in God's infallible foreknowledge but in his unchanging purpose.

Of the great medieval systematizers, none excelled Thomas, whose *Summa Theologica* has been universally recognized as one of the major treatises of systematic theology.[6] In the *Summa* Thomas sets the stage for his understanding of predestination with his treatment of the will of God (Q. 19) in twelve articles in which he affirms that God's will is the final cause of all things, that it is unchangeable, and that it is always fulfilled. He then proceeds to the topic of providence (Q. 22) and from the perspective of this doctrine elaborates his doctrine of predestination (Q. 23). Thus he treats predestination as a specific aspect of providence. "I answer that it is fitting that God should predestine [elect] men, for all things are subject to his providence, as shown above" (Q. 23, art. 1).

While this approach differs from that of Augustine, who relates predestination to the doctrine of salvation rather than of providence, Thomas agrees with Augustine on the essential matter: predestination to salvation is based not on foreseen faith but on the will of God,

---

6. The Reformers, in their reaction to Scholasticism, did not do Thomas (1225–1274) justice. Luther called him "the fountain and original soup of all heresy, error and gospel havoc, as his books bear witness" (Luther, quoted by Schaff in *History of the Christian Church*, 5: 676). Though not a seminal thinker, Thomas, the *doctor angelicus*, has enjoyed a commanding eminence because of the clarity of his method, the balance of his judgment, and the sheer scope of his analysis. In 1879, Leo XIII made his theology the standard of all Catholic teaching.

who shows mercy. Thus the salvation of the elect is not only unmerited but also certain and infallible. And, like Augustine, he thinks of the predestined as a fixed number. (In Art. 6 Thomas seems to imply that the number is the same as that of the fallen angels [following Augustine], but in Art. 7 he simply observes that some think the number of the predestined equals the number of unfallen angels or of all angels together.) Thomas departs somewhat from Augustine on the question of reprobation. God reprobates some, he suggests, but in the sense that in his providence he permits them to fall away from their true end and imposes punishment on them for their sin. God loves all persons in that he wills some good to all, but he does not will all good to all. Insofar as he does not will the particular good of eternal life to all, says Thomas, he can be said to reprobate some (Art. 3, "Whether God Reprobates Any Man").

FROM THE REFORMATION TO THE PRESENT

The position taken by Thomas reflects the essential state of the question as it was reopened at the time of the Protestant Reformation. Those who led the Reformation—Zwingli, Luther, Calvin—were all double predestinarians. As Schaff observes,

> All the Reformers of the sixteenth century, including even the gentle Melanchthon and the compromising Bucer, under a controlling sense of human depravity and saving grace, in extreme antagonism to Pelagianism and self-righteousness, and, as they sincerely believed, in full harmony not only with the greatest of the Fathers, but also with the inspired St. Paul, came to the same doctrine of a double predestination which declares the eternal destiny of all men.[7]

In reacting to the teaching of the Reformers, the Council of Trent (1563) warned against presuming that individuals can be assured they are among the predestinate, since predestination is a sacred mystery (Decree on Justification, chap. 12), and anathematized those who teach predestination to evil ("Of Justification," chap. 17). But it was the posthumous publication of Cornelius Jansen's *Augustinus* (1640) that caused the greatest furor. As a Roman Catholic

---

7. Schaff, *The History of the Creeds*, vol. 1 of *Bibliotheca symbolica ecclesiae universalis* (New York: Harper, 1877), p. 451.

bishop (Ypres) and professor of theology (Louvain) and an obvious authority on Augustine, Jansen could hardly be ignored. On May 31, 1653, Innocent X condemned five Jansenist doctrines that read like a page out of the Protestant Reformation—namely, radical depravity, predestination, efficacious grace, the loss of free will, and particular atonement. Although Pascal defended the Jansenist position in his immortal Provincial Letters, it was repeatedly condemned by subsequent popes and bitterly attacked by the Jesuits.[8]

Though Protestantism was never convulsed by such physically brutal controversy, the early unanimity of the Reformers concerning predestination was short-lived. The movement away from strict Augustinianism began with Melanchthon. In the first chapter of the first edition (1521) of his *Loci Theologici*, a landmark in theology written when he was a mere twenty-four years old, Melanchthon elaborated such a clear doctrine of divine predestination that Luther rhapsodized (in the preface to *De Servo Arbitrio*) that the work was worthy of a place in the canon. But as time went on, Melanchthon inclined more and more to the semi-Augustinian synergism of the Middle Ages and anticipated the Arminianism that was later to surface in the Reformed tradition.[9]

This mild Augustinianism is given definitive statement in Article 11 of the Lutheran Formula of Concord. There it is suggested that predestination or election, when rightly understood, consoles sinners with the assurance of God's grace apart from any merit of their own. Election means that in his eternal counsel, God has decreed that they only shall be saved who acknowledge his Son. Thus, election is solely in Christ, who earnestly desires the salvation of all, a desire that is not fulfilled because—and only because—the

---

8. In 1713 Pope Clement XI condemned 101 sentences from Jansenist writings. In the bull *Unigenitus Dei Filius* he labeled these sentences "false, captious, ill-sounding, offensive to pious ears, scandalous, blasphemous." The Port Royal Convent, a center of Jansenist influence, was abolished by the pope in 1709, the building was destroyed by Louis XIV in 1710, the corpses of illustrious saints were exhumed from the cemetery in 1711, and the church was destroyed in 1712. Many Jansenists, both monks and nuns, fled to the Netherlands. See Schaff, *The History of the Creeds*, pp. 102ff.

9. Calvin, who wrote the preface to the French edition of the *Loci* and retained a friendly relationship with Melanchthon to the end, expressed surprise in his private correspondence that so great a theologian should have come to reject the scriptural doctrine of eternal predestination.

wicked make it impossible for the Spirit effectually to work for their salvation. God does foreknow all that will come to pass, including the evil end of the wicked, the Formula continues, but this divine prescience does not cause any to perish; rather, it sets bounds to evil and in some instances even turns evil to good for the salvation of the elect.[10]

It is in the Reformed tradition, under the commanding influence of Calvin and his successor Beza, that the Augustinian doctrine of predestination has prevailed. If not the cornerstone of Calvin's thought—an exaggeration frequently heard—it is surely a fundamental plank in his theological platform. For Calvin, predestination is the eternal counsel of God by which he has, for his own glory, chosen some to eternal life and others to eternal death. The salvation of the elect reveals the depth of God's mercy, and the condemnation of the reprobate reveals the severity of his justice. Like Augustine, Calvin confesses that the whole question of God's predestination is an inscrutable mystery; but he insists that our inability to understand does not give us the right to reject the doctrine, for it is plainly revealed in Scripture. And when rightly used, it is the best antidote to Pelagianism, a genuine rebuke to human pride, and the source of unending gratitude to the God of all grace.

In the creeds and catechisms of the Reformed and Anglican traditions, the doctrine of Calvin has been freely confessed, with more or less explicit detail, depending upon the times and circumstances in which the documents have been produced. These documents, written over a period of about 150 years, from Zwingli's *Fidei Ratio* (1530) to the *Formula Consensus Helvetica* (1675), rep-

---

10. The Saxon Visitation Articles, written by Lutheran divines in 1592 (less than fifty years after Luther's death) to counteract Calvinistic "leaven" in Electoral Saxony, affirm that Christ died for all and condemn the doctrines (1) that "God created the greater part of mankind for eternal damnation," (2) that the elect can never be damned "though they commit great sins of every kind," and (3) that the nonelect "can not arrive at salvation, though they be baptized a thousand times, and receive the Eucharist every day, and lead as blameless a life as ever can be led." These articles never attained general authority in Lutheran circles.

For a summary of the controversy in American Lutheran circles, see E. Clifford Nelson, *The Lutheran Church among Norwegian-Americans* (Minneapolis: Augsburg, 1960), pp. 177ff., and *The Lutherans in North America* (Philadelphia: Fortress, 1975), pp. 313–25. In the nineteenth century some American Lutherans subscribed to predestination to salvation and faith; others, to predestination to salvation in view of faith.

resent a confessional commitment on the part of many even down to the present day.[11] As the various aspects of the doctrine are elaborated, the following themes occur with striking frequency:

1. There is a divine providence whereby God, according to his eternal counsel, upholds and governs all his creatures. Thus all things come to pass not by chance but according to God's plan and purpose.

2. At the heart of this providential purpose of God is his gracious election of some to eternal life.

3. This eternal election is in Christ, who is the mirror, as it were, in which we contemplate with gratitude our own election.

4. This election of some unto life implies the rejection of others, whose death is the death of the reprobate.

5. The choice of the elect is not based upon God's foreknowledge of their faith, much less upon their merit or desert, but wholly upon his good pleasure.

6. By contrast, those who are foreordained to death are contemplated as members of a fallen humanity whom God passes by and devotes to a just condemnation for their disobedience and unbelief.

7. Thus it is that while the salvation of the elect is due to God's grace alone, the condemnation of the reprobate is due to their sin and transgression.

8. Hence, there is no naked decree (*decretum absolutum*) whereby God condemns some according to his pleasure and wholly apart from any consideration of their deserts; much less is God the author of sin.

9. The number of the elect, known only to God, is fixed and definite and can be neither increased nor diminished.

10. Though God predestines the elect to salvation and the reprobate to condemnation, the word of the gospel is a genuine and

---

11. The most relevant texts are conveniently laid out in B. B. Warfield's "Predestination in the Reformed Confessions," in *Studies in Theology* (New York: Oxford University Press, 1932), pp. 149–218. For Congregational, Baptist, and other confessional statements on predestination, see the following: Williston Walker, *The Creeds and Platforms of Congregationalism* (Boston: Pilgrim, 1960); W. L. Lumpkin, *Baptist Confessions of Faith* (Philadelphia: Judson Press, 1959); Schaff, *The Evangelical Protestant Creeds*, vol. 3 of *Bibliotheca symbolica ecclesiae universalis*, parts 3 and 4.

sincere call to repentance, and the response to that call is a free and responsible choice both in those who accept and in those who reject the gospel.

11. This "high article" of predestination is a mystery, for God has sealed the Book of Life until the day of judgment. To those who cavil at it, one can only respond in the words of the apostle, "But who are you, a man, to answer back to God?" (Rom. 9:20).

12. The purpose of the doctrine is not to "agitate us with miserable anxiety and perturbation" but to fill us with joy, for God "has chosen us that we should be holy and without blame before him in love." Election, then, is "the foundation of every saving good."

While this doctrine of predestination became a pivotal article in the Reformed tradition, it remained a controversial one. In the course of this controversy, Calvin's celebrated admission that he found the decree—concerning the reprobate—horrible (*Inst.*, 3, 23, 7) was often cited. But in his own case and in that of his followers, this admission reflected not a sadistic turn of mind but an unshakable conviction that double predestination was the plain teaching of Scripture. Such reasoning, however, did not satisfy many, even though they accepted the authority of Scripture. In Holland, where the doctrine was given its most vigorous defense, it also suffered its most vigorous rejection in the teachings of Jacobus Arminius, which have come to be known as Arminianism.[12] Citing the twentieth question of the Heidelberg Catechism, that not all who perish in Adam are saved but those only those who "by true faith are engrafted into Christ and embrace all his benefits," Arminius comments, "From this sentence I infer that *God has not absolutely predestined any to salvation; but that he has in his decree considered (or looked upon) them as believers.*"[13] Pursuing such reasoning, Arminius came to the final conclusion that God foresees the choice

---

[12]. Born near Utrecht, Holland, in 1650, Arminius studied theology first at the University of Leyden and later under Beza, Calvin's successor, in Geneva. He was eventually appointed professor of divinity at Leyden (1603). His one-time teacher and later arch-opponent was Francis Gomarus, who also taught theology at Leyden.

[13]. Jacobus Arminius, *Writings*, 3 vols., trans. James Nichols (Grand Rapids: Baker, 1956), 1: 221; italics his. In many other places Arminius comes to a similar conclusion.

the sinner will make and bases his own choice thereon. Hence, he maintained that every scheme of predestination, and particularly the supralapsarian view of his opponent Gomarus, subverts the gospel.

After much controversy in the decade following Arminius's death, five articles were drawn up by his followers under the name of a Remonstrance. A national synod of the Dutch Church, convened at Dort on November 13, 1618, not only rejected the Arminian articles but affirmed five counterdoctrines which the Arminians rejected in turn. These five doctrines came to be known as the five points of Calvinism (commonly remembered with the help of the acronym TULIP): (1) total (radical) depravity, (2) unconditional election, (3) limited (particular) atonement, (4) irresistible (efficacious) grace, and (5) perseverance of the saints.[14]

While Dutch Arminianism tended through the years to move toward the latitudinarian theology of Liberalism—the Fatherhood of God, the brotherhood of humankind, the leadership of Jesus— the original Arminian doctrine of free will became influential in Britain. As for the Church of England, Article 17 of the Thirty-Nine Articles, the article on predestination, is so obviously Calvinistic that early efforts (from about 1590) to give it a compromised interpretation met with strong opposition and came to nought. However, the countereffort to give the Calvinistic doctrine a full-blown statement in the Lambeth Articles (1595) provoked sufficient resistance that these Articles never attained general symbolical authority in the Anglican Church.

Meanwhile the high-church, Tractarian interpretation of Article 17 identified election with ecclesiastical calling and the elect with the baptized. This interpretation so strained the spirit and letter of the original that it never gained a wide assent. However, the renewal of interest in sacramental grace which Tractarianism brought

---

14. Though the debate with the Remonstrants principally concerned these doctrines related to predestination, other items in Arminius's thought were also discussed and rejected. Though generally forgotten long since, some of these items anticipated the subsequent radical departure of his followers from Protestant orthodoxy. Arminius, for example, defended the thesis that "It is a new, heretical and Sabellian mode of speaking, nay, it is blasphemous to say [as Calvin] that the Son of God is *homoousios* (very God), for the Father alone is very God, not the Son or the Spirit"; or again, "The righteousness of Christ is not imputed to us for righteousness [as Luther contends] but to believe (or the act of believing) justifies us" (see Arminius, *Writings*, 1: 339, 355).

to the Anglican communion and the concomitant appeal to Augustine's sacramentalism *in contrast to* the evangelical strand of his thought (which was the basis of Calvinism) inevitably came to divide the English Church on the issue of predestination.

In the meantime, the Methodist movement became sharply divided over the question of predestination, even while it was a part of the Anglican communion. Both George Whitefield and John Wesley,[15] the founders of Methodism, were Anglican priests and therefore members of a communion that was confessionally Calvinistic. Under the influence of Jonathan Edwards, Whitefield became personally committed to Calvinism. But his friend Wesley, the real organizer and moving spirit behind the Methodist movement, saw things differently. A man inclined to think an emphasis on doctrine more divisive than helpful, he omitted Article 17 altogether when he abridged the Thirty-Nine Articles for the use of his followers. As

---

15. See, for instance, his sermon 54, "On Free Grace (Rom. 8:32)," preached at Bristol: "Call it, therefore, by whatever name you please, election, preterition, predestination, or reprobation, it comes in the end to the same thing." His brother Charles gave his antipathy for the doctrine poetic expression in the lines:

O horrible decree,
    Worthy of whence it came!
Forgive their hellish blasphemy,
    Who blame it on the Lamb.

Augustus Toplady, a devout Anglican and ardent Calvinist, at the tender age of nineteen had translated from the Latin, for his private edification, Jerome Zanchius's *Absolute Predestination*. When John Wesley published somewhat mutilated extracts from this book over Toplady's initials, the latter became so incensed that he published the entire work in English with a preface. In this preface he declared that God's sovereign will, unalterable decree, and all-active providence constituted the great three-linked chain of divine causes: (1) the stream of God's providence flows (2) in the channel of his decree, arising (3) in the adorable spring of his will.

> Were I concerned in drawing up an expurgatory index to language, I would, without mercy, cashier and proscribe such words as chance, fortune, luck, casualty, contingency, and mishap. Nor unjustly. For they are . . . mere terms without ideas. Absolute expletives which import nothing. Unmeaning cyphers, either proudly designed to hide man's ignorance of real causes, or sacrilegiously designed to rob the Deity of the honors due to his wisdom, providence and power. (*Absolute Predestination* [rpt.; Evansville: Sovereign Grace Book Club, 1960], p. 21)

Today Methodists do not sing Wesley's hymn on the horrible decree, but they do sing Toplady's "Rock of Ages." And of course Presbyterians and everyone else sing Wesley's "Jesus, Lover of My Soul." Theologically speaking, it would seem that the hymnbook is the church's supreme ecumenical achievement.

the controversy with Whitefield and the Calvinistic Methodists who followed him heated up, Wesley thundered against the horrors of the doctrine of unconditional election in his sermons. (This thunder continued to resound from Methodist pulpits until the rise of religious liberalism removed the thunder from many a Methodist pulpit altogether.) The irresistible decree, as Wesley styled it, which infallibly secures the salvation of the elect and the damnation of the reprobate, makes preaching useless, enervates zeal for good works, and turns God into a hypocrite.

Wesley's rejection of predestination was—fortunately—more emotional than critical. Not given to the rigors of thought of which dogmatics is made, he never pursued the implications of his Arminian view of salvation. While he gave the decision and choice of the creature precedence over the decision and choice of the Redeemer, he remained quite Augustinian in his view of sin. Original sin was not simply moral weakness for Wesley, as for the classic Arminians, but a depravity that requires the grace of God for salvation. His descriptions of the fall were as dark as any of those found in Augustine, Luther, or Calvin. Correspondingly, he thought of conversion as a work of grace in the radical sense, and in his preaching he stressed the need to be "born again." Wesleyan Arminianism remained, therefore, much more evangelical than that of the Dutch Remonstrants, and this evangelical Arminianism is still vital in certain circles of contemporary Methodism.

In Protestant Liberalism, to continue our brief historical overview, the so-called "problem of predestination" does not really exist, since latitudinarianism is entailed in its inclusivist approach to all theological issues. When Christianity is defined in terms of the "universal Fatherhood of God and the brotherhood of man" and when "salvation by character" is a viable prospect secured through "the progress of the human race onward and upward forever," then all the traditional concepts of Christian thought, including predestination, are given new meaning.

As the first major spokesman for Protestant Liberalism, Schleiermacher restates the doctrine of predestination in a significant way. He understands election to mean that in accordance with the laws of divine government, those living on earth at one time are never uniformly taken up into the kingdom of God. When individuals are taken up into that kingdom, each in his or her own turn, this is

ELECTION AND PREDESTINATION

> simply the result of the fact that the justifying divine activity is in manifestation determined by, and forms part of, the general government of the world. . . . And since the whole government of the world is, like the world itself, eternal in God, nothing happens in the kingdom of grace without divine fore-ordination.[16]

But the fact that there are those in whom God's predestination has not yet attained its true end (blessedness in Christ) does not allow us to conclude that for some there may be a predestination of an opposite sort, says Schleiermacher: such a conclusion would constitute an "insoluble discord," for it would mean that part of the human race is by death forever excluded from the fellowship of the kingdom. (Schleiermacher's system does not allow for "insoluble discords"—which some have called the "paradoxes of faith.")

The truth, he contends, is that all are embraced with those of us who are in the church under the same divine predestination.

> We may conclude that if only everyone who has lagged behind us is some time or another taken up into the living fellowship with Christ, our sympathetic concern can accept the fact [that not all are presently in such fellowship] with perfect satisfaction without any contradiction arising between it and our God-consciousness. (P. 542)

Hence to speak of those who have been "passed over" is fitting only in the sense that *"they appear to us to be passed over"* (p. 548).

> It is, therefore, only as it were in an appendix, not here strictly relevant, that we can deal with the other idea of there being a twofold foreordination—on the one hand to blessedness, on the other to damnation. . . . If, however, we proceed on the definite assumption that all belonging to the human race are eventually taken up into living fellowship with Christ, there is nothing for it but this single divine foreordination. (P. 549)

Of course for those who "proceed on the opposite assumption (as is obviously done in our Confessions), namely, that death is the end of the divine gracious working [in some], the proposition given above

---

16. Schleiermacher, *The Christian Faith*, ed. H. R. Mackintosh and J. S. Stewart (Edinburgh: T. & T. Clark, 1928), p. 547. Subsequent references to this volume will be cited parenthetically in the text. For a fuller discussion, see his *Über die Lehre von der Erwahlung*, in *Sammtliche Werke* (Berlin: G. Reiweis, 1836), pp. 393–484.

ceases to be a fitting statement" (p. 549). "If the matter is to end there, the logicality of Calvin's formula" — Schleiermacher says nothing of its scriptural character — "incontestably ought to be preferred" (p. 551).

We will conclude our historical overview by moving beyond theological Liberalism, which reduced the traditional discussion of election to an irrelevant "appendix," to a consideration of a theology based not upon religious feeling but upon divine revelation. Barth and Brunner, two of the spokesmen for this new approach, were members of the Swiss Reformed Church. Not surprisingly, then, they discussed the doctrine of predestination (including the questions of the divine decree, providence, election, reprobation, and even infra- and supralapsarianism) at considerable length.[17] They never questioned the centrality and importance of the doctrine, nor did they waver in their effort (not always satisfying) to be truly Reformed and biblical in their conclusions. Because we shall interact with their thought and the thought of those who followed them in our own exposition of the subject, we shall here simply sketch, in briefest compass, the way in which Barth sought to break new ground in dealing with a problem that has commanded the best efforts of the best theological minds since the days of Augustine.

In fundamental sympathy with the Augustinian position that salvation is the gift of God's electing grace rather than a reward for human merit, Barth nonetheless felt constrained to reject the traditional form in which the doctrine of predestination had been cast. Though he found it hard to believe, he became convinced that even such consummate theological minds as Augustine, Thomas, and Calvin had erred in their formulations of this doctrine. The nature of their mistake, he believed, was that they divorced God from Jesus Christ — that is to say, when they thought of God's election, they thought abstractly of the eternal decree of the hidden God rather than concretely of the gracious purpose of the God revealed in Jesus Christ. As a result, they missed the decisive insight into the heart of the matter, which has to do with the question of the object of

---

17. A convenient summary of Barth's position is found in G. C. Berkouwer's *The Triumph of Grace in the Theology of Karl Barth* (Grand Rapids: William B. Eerdmans, 1956), pp. 89–122. Berkouwer devotes an entire volume of his own to the subject of election in *Divine Election*, trans. Hugo Becker, Studies in Dogmatics (Grand Rapids: William B. Eerdmans, 1960).

predestination (*objectum praedestinationis*). All parties concerned assumed that the object of the decree was a fixed number of elect and reprobate individuals.

Barth maintained that if the theologians had thought of election and reprobation in terms of God's eternal purpose in Jesus Christ, they would have perceived that the answer to the election/reprobation question lies in him. He is the electing God who has become the elect Man—not *an* elect man among many but *the* elect Man. And all individual men and women are elect in him, the second Adam, in whom all are made alive (1 Cor. 15:22). But his election, unlike ours, is unto death, that we who deserve death might enjoy eternal life. As the One predestined to death, he is the one true Reprobate. When we speak of Christ's death, says Barth, we speak of the "shadow side of predestination." Predestination, then, is double, since Christ is both the elect Man and the reprobate Man. Double predestination in this sense, so far from being a *decretum horribile*, is really good news, since it tells us that he stands in our place as the Reprobate while we, because we are elect in him, have eternal life. This is the sum of the gospel. Thus election becomes the best of all words that can be said or heard, for it testifies to the free, unchanging grace of God, a grace to which witness is born in all his works.

Barth's effort has been praised as a breakthrough, a brilliant stroke that cuts the Gordian knot of the age-old predestinarian problem. As a landscape artist may leave the natural features of the terrain untouched yet alter the whole prospect with a rearrangement of the flora, so Barth has transformed the theological terrain of predestination by a rearrangement of the component parts of the problem. Where there was darkness, there is now light; where there was mystery, there is now good news. It did not take some theologians long, however, to perceive that Barth had solved one problem (reprobation) by introducing another (restitutionism, *apokatastasis*). If all are elect in Christ by an eternal decree, then it would seem that no negative decision at the human level (unbelief) could ever frustrate the prior positive decision at the divine level (election). Hence all will be saved in the end.

Brunner, whose theological efforts were closely associated with those of Barth, once commented that, for all he had said, Barth surely had not spoken the last word on election. Of Brunner's own "existential" approach to the question of election we shall have more to say in our subsequent exposition. In the present survey we have been concerned simply to indicate the contours of the discussion, which have been evolving from the days of the Augustinian/Pelagian controversy to the present.

Addendum
The Place of the Doctrine in Systematics

As we conclude this historical sketch, we should make a brief comment on the question of order, a question that always confronts the systematician. Where, in dogmatics, does the exposition of the doctrine of predestination belong? Augustine, as we have seen, assumed that election is a part of soteriology. Morally incapacitated by the fall, the descendants of Adam no longer have the freedom to choose the good. The fact that some do is attributable to God's electing grace. Even faith is a gift bestowed on those who are chosen in Christ from before the foundation of the world. Salvation, then, is wholly of grace according to Augustine.

Aquinas held that election and reprobation are special instances of a general providence. His argument moves directly from the consideration of God's providence (*Summa Theologica*, Q. 22) to predestination (Q. 23). "As men are ordained to eternal life through the providence of God," he states, "it is likewise a part of that providence to permit some to fall away" (Art. 3).

Calvin places the discussion of predestination at the close of the doctrine of salvation (*Inst.*, 3, 21–24) as a kind of bridge to the discussion of the church, which is the assembly of the elect, the *coetus electorum*. (Actually Calvin located election in four different places, if one takes into account earlier editions of the *Institutes* and other writings such as the Gallican Confession).

Beza, Calvin's successor at Geneva, treats of predestination under the topic of providence, as did Thomas. It is likely that he placed the doctrine so centrally in his writings because he felt he had to defend Calvin's thought on this point above all others. But what was a historical matter in Beza's case tends to become a *principium* in later Reformed dogmatics. In what is sometimes called "scholastic Calvinism," the concept of the divine decree tends to become not just an important theological theme but a basic metaphysical principle. All God's works of creation and providence are understood to be the unfolding of the divine decree.

Some have complained that such a position seems to imply that, given the knowledge of the divine attributes, such "decretal theology," if consistently applied, would enable one to arrive at the entire content of systematics by a simple deduction from the doctrine of God.

> Chained to his throne a volume lies,
> With all the fates of men,
> With every angel's form and size
> Drawn by the eternal pen.
> —Watts

In my judgment, this complaint is clearly overdrawn.[18] For all the difference of emphasis, there is a fundamental continuity between the thought of the Reformers and their Calvinistic successors in the matter of predestination.

Barth acknowledges the seeming similarity between this decretal theology and his own decision to place the doctrine of election before the doctrines of creation, providence, and salvation. But he is careful to point out the difference. He is not concerned with a *general* decree of universal predestination (*decretum Dei generale*)—what the Westminster divines describe as God's foreordination of "whatever comes to pass"—but the special decree (*decretum Dei speciale*) of election and reprobation. Nevertheless, the place he gives to the doctrine puts him squarely in the company of the supralapsarians. Of course Barth seeks to escape the moral problem with traditional supralapsarianism (the affirmation that God created the reprobate to be damned) by limiting the number of the reprobate to precisely one individual, Jesus Christ, who, though he "descended into hell," yet triumphed in the end when, on the third day, he "rose again from the dead."

Whatever the merits of Barth's position, it fails in the judgment of many, as we have observed, to resolve the essential problem, and so it also fails to resolve the secondary question of placement. But though Barth's word is not the last theologically, it may be considered the last of historical significance. And so we shall conclude the addendum to our historical survey at this point and turn to the exposition of the doctrine.

---

18. For more on this matter, see Richard Muller, *Christ and the Decree* (Durham: Labyrinth Press, 1984).

2
The Biblical Data Summarized

Unlike the word *Trinity*, the word *election* reflects the language of Scripture itself.[1] To speak of "election" is to speak of a concept rooted in the Old Testament teaching, that out of the whole human family God chose Abraham, Sarah, and their descendants to be his unique people. Israel is that blessed nation whose God is the Lord, the people whom he has chosen (בחר) as his heritage (Ps. 33:12). This idea of a chosen people is carried over into the New Testament, though not in terms of a nation as such. Rather, the followers of Jesus from among all nations who confess him as Lord and repent of their sins are the New Israel, God's elect. It matters not whether they are Jews or Gentiles, for in Christ there is neither Jew nor Greek (Gal. 3:28).

Jesus made three interesting statements concerning the elect: first, he declared that God will "vindicate his elect, who cry to him day and night" (Luke 18:7); second, he said that the trials of the end time will be shortened "for the sake of the elect" (Matt. 24:22); and third, he promised that in that day, when false Christs shall seek to deceive "the elect" (Mark 13:22), the Son of Man shall deliver them, sending his angels to "gather his elect from the four winds, from the ends of the earth to the ends of heaven" (Mark 13:27). Likewise, Paul speaks out about it. "Who," he asks, "shall bring any charge against God's elect?" (Rom. 8:33). In his first letter to the Thessa-

---

1. Latin *electio*, from the verb *eligere*, translating εκλογη (Heb. בחר), "to choose," "to select," "to pick out."

lonians he gives thanks to God for them, knowing that they have been "chosen" (1 Thess. 1:2–4). He admonishes the Colossians to put on compassion as "God's chosen" (Col. 3:12). He describes himself as "an apostle of Jesus Christ, to further the faith of God's elect" (Titus 1:1), and as such he endures "everything for the sake of the elect," that they also may obtain salvation (2 Tim. 2:10). Admonishing us to consider our calling as Christians, he reminds us that God has elected (chosen) what is foolish in the world in order to shame the wise, what is weak in order to shame the strong, the things that are not in order to bring to nought the things that are (1 Cor. 1:27–28). In the same vein, James reminds his readers that God has elected those who are poor in this world to be rich in faith and heirs of his promised kingdom (James 2:5). And when, according to the seer's vision, that kingdom shall come in glory and the Lamb who is King of kings and Lord of lords shall celebrate his victory, they who are "called and chosen and faithful" shall be with him (Rev. 17:14).

Few, indeed, are those who today speak as these Scriptures do, so far have we drifted from the biblical moorings of our faith regarding the doctrine of election. But in New Testament times it was not so. Even when they did not use the word "election" ($εκλογη$), it was natural for the early Christians to speak of God as the electing God. James, for example, in his crucial address to the Jerusalem council, reminds his hearers, "Symeon has related how God first visited the Gentiles, to *take out* of them a people ($λαβειν\ εξ\ εθνων\ λαον$) for his name" (Acts 15:14). This account of the Gentile mission reminds one of the way Paul spoke to his converts in Thessalonica, the fruit of his first mission journey: "We are bound to give thanks to God always for you . . . because God chose you from the beginning to be saved" (2 Thess. 2:13). On his second missionary journey, the apostle's courage was buoyed by a vision of the Lord assuring him "I have many people in this city" (Acts 18:10). Such a way of speaking was fully in harmony with the way the Lord had spoken on a previous occasion when he addressed his Father as he who had empowered him "to give eternal life to all whom thou hast given him" (John 17:2, 6, 9, 24). Among those "given him" were people in Corinth, to whom the apostle as God's ambassador proceeded in due time to bring the words of eternal life.

That this divine election is according to God's will is manifest from the use of a whole congeries of terms in Scripture, variously translated "to destine," "to ordain," "to appoint," "to decree," "to determine," in which God is the acting Subject. As he has determined (οριζω) the times and bounds of those he has created and placed on earth (Acts 17:26), so, Luke tells us, he has "ordained to eternal life" (οσοι ησαν τεταγμενοι εις ζωην αιωνιον) the Gentiles in Pisidian Antioch who believed when Paul and Barnabas preached to them (Acts 13:48). Accordingly, God's election and his "purpose" are closely conjoined. (This purpose, in the literal phrase of Rom. 9:11, is "an-according-to-election-purpose," η κατ' εκλογην προθεσις). And this electing purpose is projected back into eternity with the use of such verbs as "predestinate" or "foreordain." God not only "destines" but predestines; he not only ordains but *fore*-ordains. Thus, the divine will, though it by no means annuls the human will, is given preeminence. As Paul says, "Those whom [God] foreknew he also predestined [προωρισεν] to be conformed to the image of his Son" (Rom. 8:29). God has elected us in Christ "before the foundation of the world" (προ καταβολης κοσμου), "having destined us in love to be his sons . . . according to the counsel of his will" (προορισας ημας . . . κατα την ευδοκιαν του θεληματος αυτου, Eph. 1:4–5, 11). And so he saves us not according to our works but according to his purpose and grace, which were given us in Christ Jesus "ages ago" (προ χρονων αιωνιων, 2 Tim. 1:9).

Election obviously implies rejection. When the early disciples asked the Lord to choose (literally "to elect," εξελεξω, Acts 1:24) a successor to Judas in the apostolate, his election of Matthias involved the rejection of Justus (Acts 1:26). Likewise the Seven were elected (εξελεξαντο) out of "the whole multitude" of the faithful (Acts 6:5). Of course such choices to a given task are hardly as "laden with eternity" as election to eternal salvation, and so there has never been a reason for anyone to doubt the implications of rejection at such a mundane level. But when the choice *is* laden with eternity, theologians have understandably been much more concerned with the implications. If the scriptural language of election sounds unfamiliar to our ears, surely the language of rejection sounds even more so. Yet such language is too prominent and persistent in Scripture to be simply edited out of the vocabulary of contemporary theological discourse.

When asked by the disciples why he spoke in parables, Jesus gave the surprising answer that the mystery of the kingdom is not given to all. There are those who are "outside" (εκεινοις δε τοις εξω, Mark 4:11), and, he explained, he had to speak to them in parables in order that they indeed might see but not perceive, and that they might hear but not understand (Mark 4:12).[2] Similarly surprising is the prayer Jesus offered as he exulted in the Spirit: "I thank thee, Father, . . . that thou hast hidden these things from the wise and understanding . . ., yea, Father, for so it was well pleasing to thee" (Luke 10:21; see Matt. 11:25–27). Surprising, too, is John's comment on the unbelief of many of Jesus' hearers: he says they "*could not* believe" (ουκ ηδυναντο πιστευειν, John 12:39), in fulfillment of the prophecy that God would blind their eyes and harden their hearts (Isa. 6:10). This way of putting the matter corresponds to the Johannine report of Jesus' answer to unbelieving Jews gathered for the Feast of Dedication in the Portico of Solomon: "You do not believe, because you do not belong to my sheep" (John 10:26). Most would find it easier to understand him were he to say, "You do not belong to my sheep because you do not believe."

Mysterious as it may be, the rejection implicit in the concept of election is also a part of the purpose of him who accomplishes all things according to the counsel of his will. God is the God who not only has mercy on whom he will, but also hardens whom he will (αρα ουν ον θελει ελεει, ον δε θελει σκληρυνει, Rom. 9:18). As God's election obtains the salvation of some in Israel, so the rest are "hardened" by him who gives them "a spirit of stupor, eyes that they should not see and ears that they should not hear, down to this very day" (Rom. 11:7–8). In a similar vein, we might note that Christ is not only the elect and precious Cornerstone in Zion but also a Stone of Offense against which the disobedient stumble "as they were destined to do" (εις ο και ετεθησαν, 1 Pet. 2:6–8). These disobedient ones threaten "the faith which was once for all delivered to the saints,... who long ago were designated" (KJV, "before of old ordained") to this condemnation (Jude 3–4).[3]

---

2. This meaning also comes through in the parallel in Luke 8:9–10, but in Matthew 13:13 it reads simply "because seeing they see not" (KJV, RSV).

3. Literally, "those of old having been written before to this condemnation" (οι παλαι προγεγραμμενοι εις τουτο το κριμα)—an instance of the so-called "prophetic necessity." What is written in the prophets must come to pass. See C. L. W. Grimm, *A Greek-English Lexicon of the New Testament*, trans. Joseph H. Thayer (1887; Grand Rapids: Zondervan, 1977), s.v. δει, e. See also the text mentioned above, "they could not believe" (John 12:39) because of what was written in Isaiah 6:10.

While the preaching of the apostles confirms the mystery of election and rejection in a striking fashion, in that some who heard them believed and others did not, at the same time the record of this preaching confronts us with genuine difficulties. In the historical *reporting* in Acts of what happened when the apostles preached, the life-and-death importance of the *human* choice is presented as being preeminent: one's salvation or condemnation appears to depend on whether one believes or disbelieves the gospel. But in the theological *interpretation* of what happened given in the epistles, the *divine* choice is presented as being preeminent. How are these two perspectives related? Paul (whose preaching split more than one synagogue), speaking in the figure of a Roman triumph, describes his ministry (and himself the minister) as a fragrance from death to death on the one hand, and from life to life on the other (2 Cor. 2:14−16).[4] Yet he goes on to make a comment that any theologian who has wrestled with the problem of election can appreciate: "And who is sufficient for these things?" How true.

Perhaps we can find a sufficient answer in the prayer of Augustine: "Give what thou commandest and command what thou wilt." God is the God who in the kerygma commands all men and women everywhere to repent, as Paul announced to the Athenians (Acts 17:30), but he is also the God who gives repentance to some, as the early Jewish Christians acknowledged after hearing of Peter's mission to the house of Cornelius (Acts 11:18). Thus, to those for whom the gospel is "a savor of life unto life" God gives what he commands. But what of those for whom the gospel is a "savor of death unto death"? If God has given *them* a spirit of stupor, eyes that should not see, and ears that should not hear down to this very day (Rom. 11:8; Isa. 29:10), how, in their case, shall we understand the imperative "Believe in the Lord Jesus Christ" (Acts 16:31), with which the apostles confronted all to whom they preached? In their case, it would seem, God commands what he does not give and gives what he does not command.

Even more perplexing, if possible, is the content of the kerygma itself. The apostles preached a message that not only imposed

---

4. "From death to death" meaning from the death of Christ proclaimed to the death of the sinner who spurns that proclamation, and "from life to life" meaning from the resurrection of Christ proclaimed to the life of the sinner who accepts that proclamation.

THE BIBLICAL DATA SUMMARIZED

the obligation on all to repent and believe the gospel, but assured all who came within earshot that God in Christ was "reconciling the *world* to himself, not counting their trespasses against them" (2 Cor. 5:19). This reconciliation was effected by him "whose act of righteousness leads to acquittal and life for *all*," for "by [his] obedience *many* will be made righteous" (Rom. 5:18–19). This act of righteous obedience culminated in his death on a Roman cross. As Christ crucified, "he is the propitiation for our sins; and not for ours only, but also for the sins of the whole world" (1 John 2:2, ASV). To this "Lamb of God, who takes away the sin of the world" (John 1:29), to this "man Christ Jesus, who gave himself as a ransom for all" (1 Tim. 2:5–6) the apostles bore eloquent witness in due time. And so through their witness the grace of God appeared for the salvation of all (Titus 2:11), even the grace of the God who will have all men and women to be saved (1 Tim. 2:4)—the God who "so loved the world that he gave his only Son" (John 3:16), because he is "not wishing that any should perish, but that all should reach repentance" (2 Pet. 3:9).[5]

This summary of Scripture, cursory as it has been, makes it abundantly clear that there are problems with the biblical doctrine of salvation that are not of the theologian's making. How are we to understand the relation of the divine choice to the human choice? And, at a deeper level, how are we to understand God's choice as both particular, electing some and rejecting others, and at the same time universal, desiring all to be saved and to that end enjoining all to believe? These are questions that the theologians have found difficult, as our historical overview of the predestination controversy has made all too clear. At the same time they are questions that Christians cannot avoid when they reflect upon their faith. The difficulties inevitably present themselves to all who study the Scriptures and to all who ponder their own experience of the grace of salvation. And so it is with diffidence, yet with a sense of urgency, that we turn to the task before us: an exposition of the doctrine of election.

---

5. The fact that in this passage the verb is βουλομαι, whereas in Romans 9:18 it is θελω contributes nothing to the resolution of the question of how the God who hardens whom he will, can at the same time will that all repent. (For a lexical comment on the meaning of the two verbs, see Grimm, *A Greek-English Lexicon of the New Testament*, s.v. θελω, fin.)

3
Election and the People of God

God's covenant love was first manifested in his choice of Israel. The root of the biblical doctrine of election is the concept that Israel, as God's chosen people, is the object of his unmerited love. Aware as they were that God's love could not be grounded in their own worth, Israel's self-understanding was summed up in the words of Deuteronomy: "You are a people holy to the LORD your God, and the LORD has chosen you to be a people for his own possession, out of all the peoples that are on the face of the earth" (Deut. 14:2, cf. 7:6). Hence, in the oracle of Balaam they are described as "a people dwelling alone, and not reckoning itself among the nations" (Num. 23:9). If *covenant* is the central word in Israel's vocabulary, it is hardly too much to say that *election* is the word that gives the covenant its distinctive meaning. The covenant made with Israel is not a contract between equals but a sovereign and free promise of salvation grounded in the mysterious choice and decision of Yahweh to be Israel's God.

> But you, Israel, my servant,
>   Jacob, whom I have chosen, . . .
> you whom I took from the ends of the earth,
>   and called from its farthest corners,
> saying to you, "You are my servant,
>   I have chosen you and not cast you off";
> fear not, for I am with you,
>   be not dismayed, for I am your God. (Isa. 41:8–10)

To be sure, Israel's election implies the rejection of other peoples. Hence, Israel is duly warned against any form of religious syncretism. With their neighbors who worship false gods, they are to make no marriages, lest they be turned away from following the LORD. They are to break down their altars, dash in pieces their pillars, hew down their Asherim, and burn their graven images with fire (Deut. 7:1–5). But the LORD's choice of Israel was not intended to establish a purely negative polarity between Israel and the other nations of the earth. On the contrary, from the very beginning God chose Abraham and Sarah that in their offspring all the families of the earth should bless themselves (Gen. 22:18; 26:4). To be sure, the concept of election was sometimes politicized into a narrow nationalism (witness Jonah's attitude toward Nineveh, Jon. 3:10–4:1), but its true intent was that the chosen people should be the LORD's witnesses. " 'You are my witnesses,' says the LORD, 'and my servant whom I have chosen, that you may know and believe me and understand that I am He' " (Isa. 43:10). In this prophecy Israel's restoration becomes a witness to all nations, a "light to the people" in order that God's salvation should reach to the ends of the earth (Isa. 49:6).[1]

THE CHURCH THE HEIR OF ISRAEL'S ELECTION

This Old Testament doctrine of the election of Israel is carried over into the New and applied to the church. Hence, in the words of the familiar hymn, Christians sing,

> Ye chosen seed of Israel's race,
> Ye ransomed from the fall,
> Hail him who saves you by his grace
> And crown him Lord of all.
> —*Perronet*

---

1. This so-called "teleological" approach to election, an approach that emphasizes that those who are elect are elect and chosen for a task, is not meant to explain election in a logical fashion; the teaching that God elects individuals to a task or office *supplements* but does not take the place of the doctrine of election to salvation. It is important to note this point in light of the unconvincing arguments of such scholars as H. H. Rowley, who affirms that God chose Israel to reveal the truth to all nations even as he chose Greece to advance civilization and culture. He contends that if we adopt this approach to election we can avoid the horns of the dilemma that if God chooses the worthy, his grace is impugned, whereas if he chooses the unworthy, his justice is impugned (see *The Biblical Doctrine of Election* [London: Lutterworth, 1950], pp. 39ff.).

How did this belief that the Christian church is the heir of Israel's election come about? The answer is implicit in the Old Testament itself. Israel is elect and chosen to bear witness to the truth in order that all people may know and worship the true God. This entails the thought that members of other nations might become members of the elect community (as Ruth the Moabite) even though they were not born into the nation of Israel as such. It also entails the thought that those who were biological descendants of Abraham and Sarah could not rely on the accident of birth while repudiating the covenant by an ungodly life. Should they do so, though they might boast that they were elect, were members of the chosen race, theirs would be a vain and empty confidence. If they failed, in the words of 2 Peter 1:10, to "be the more zealous to confirm your call and election," they would forfeit their status and privilege as members in the covenant.

It is this flexibility in defining the people of God even in the Old Testament that led to the doctrine of the Remnant (see, for example, Isa. 6:9–13; 7:3; 8:2, 18; 9:12). The Remnant comprises the true people of God, who are the descendants of Abraham regardless of their natural pedigree, because of their faithfulness to the covenant.[2] In turn, the doctrine of the Remnant becomes the basis of the New Testament supposition that the elect community is made up of those who walk in the steps of Abraham's faith, whether they be Jews or Gentiles. Hence, the conclusion of the writers of the New Testament that those who embrace the covenant as newly mediated in Christ are God's chosen people is quite in keeping with the theology of the Old Testament.

This understanding of the Old Testament by the writers of the New is reflected in the warning of Jesus, attached to the parable of the wicked husbandmen, that the kingdom would be taken away from them (his unbelieving Jewish hearers) and given to a nation that would bring forth the fruits thereof (Matt. 21:43). If the church is the "nation" that inherits the kingdom belonging to Israel, then

---

2. The remnant theme is found in several of the prophets. Sometimes it designates those who survive a particular calamity (historical remnant) and sometimes those among Israel who are the true beneficiaries of salvation, especially after the exile (eschatological remnant). Isaiah was particularly interested in the latter, naming his son "Shear-Jashub," meaning "The Salvation of the Remnant" (see s.v. "Reste," *Vocabulaire de théologie biblique* (Paris: Cerf, 1962).

the church must inherit the election belonging to Israel. As Israel was, so the church now is the elect community.

For Paul such a conclusion was quite in harmony with the history of Israel from the beginning. As election had excluded some of Abraham's physical seed—Isaac was chosen rather than Ishmael, and Jacob rather than Esau (Rom. 9:6–13)—so now it includes Gentiles who are not his physical seed. These are the Gentiles who walk in Abraham's faith and thus are his heirs according to the election of grace. These believing Gentiles, together with the Jews, are the true "Israel of God" (Gal. 6:16), which is the church. Hence Paul, in speaking to the members of the Ephesian congregation, reminds them that they have been chosen from before the foundation of the world unto holiness and predestined in love to be his sons and daughters in order that through the church God's manifold wisdom might be made known to principalities and powers in heavenly places (Eph. 1:4, 5; 3:10). In the same way, Peter speaks of the church as "a chosen race, a royal priesthood, a holy nation, God's own people," whose task it is to declare the excellence of him who called them out of darkness into his marvelous light (1 Pet. 2:9).

Behind this way of speaking is an assumption that was made by all the earliest Christians who were Jews—namely, the assumption that they stood within the covenant community of Israel, that they had by no means ceased to be Jews in becoming Christians. ("Are they Hebrews? So am I. Are they Israelites? So am I," 2 Cor. 11:22). Rather, they were the heirs of God's electing grace as the true Remnant who acknowledged the fulfillment of the covenant promise in Jesus Christ and had been faithful to that covenant by sharing it with the Gentiles.

We are quite aware that the present-day rabbinate rejects the contention that Jews can confess the Christian faith and still consider themselves Jews. The Northern California Board of Rabbis, speaking of the "Jews for Jesus" movement, declared, "Their protestations to the contrary notwithstanding, they are apostates and entirely outside of the Jewish community. To claim otherwise can only be based on total ignorance." In the same statement the rabbis observed, "There are few intolerances inherent in the Jewish tradition. Only one version of it has remained constant. It is toward those who have turned away from our religious heritage in favor of another religion."[3] One

---

3. *San Francisco Jewish Bulletin*, 31 March 1972.

can only deplore the fact that the same intolerance has traditionally been shown by the church toward Christian Jews who wished to retain anything from their Jewish heritage. Such "ungenuine proselytes," as they were sometimes called, were often the victims of the inquisitorial courts of the church, especially in medieval Spain.

Sharing the covenant blessings with the Gentiles did not always come easily for the early Jews who were Christians: witness Peter's struggle as he first preached to the Gentiles of Cornelius's house (Acts 10—11:18). By the same token, the fact that their fellow Jews who refused to acknowledge Jesus as the Messiah had thereby proven themselves no longer the objects of God's electing grace was a matter of great sorrow to them. But in the end the New Testament is clear enough: the early Christians, for all their Jewish antecedents, believed that the church, including the Gentiles, was the true people of God, the heir of Israel's election.

WHAT OF THE JEWISH PEOPLE?

1. The Traditional Answer

The assumption of the early Christians that they were the heirs of Israel's election was inextricably bound up with their common confession that Jesus was the promised Messiah, the Son of the living God (Matt. 16:16). His life, death, and resurrection fulfilled the covenant promise of salvation that God had made to Israel, his chosen people. Since they were the beneficiaries of that promised salvation, they understood themselves to be the heirs of the covenant and, as such, the chosen people of God. That they were right in reaching this conclusion about themselves is the assumption on which the ensuing discussion is based. Clearly this assumption was not shared by the majority of the Jews when the Christian church emerged, any more than it is today. However, rather than attempting to examine the question of whether the early Christians were right — a matter far too complex to discuss at this juncture — we will simply assume that they were in fact correct, and on that basis seek to answer the more modest yet still difficult question this assumption forces all Christians to consider — namely, What is the status of God's ancient people the Jews? What is implied about them by the church's understanding of itself as the *coetus electorum*, the assembly of the elect? It has been all too easy, in answering this question, for theologians to assume that inasmuch as the church is the heir of Israel's election, the rejection of Israel must be final and irrevocable. To revamp the familiar Pauline figure, it is often assumed that a new olive tree has been planted in place of the old rather than that new (wild) branches were grafted onto the original stock (Rom. 11:17 – 18). This God-is-through-with-the-Jews attitude has reinforced the conflict between synagogue and church and greatly exacerbated the anti-Semitism that has scarred the soul of the Christian community.

In the comments on Romans that Luther prepared for his early lectures at Wittenberg, he clearly understood Paul (Rom. 9 – 11) to teach that God's electing purpose for Israel could not be frustrated by their unbelief. The apostle was himself evidence that God had not cast away his people whom he foreknew (11:1 – 2). The Jews, though they had fallen, would rise again, Luther maintained, encouraged by the example of the Gentiles. Hence those are "amazingly stupid" who exalt themselves "and call the Jews either dogs or accursed, or insult them with other abusive words, though they know not what kind of people they are and what is their standing in God's sight. May God resist them."[4] Luther granted that since the time of the apostles there were few Jews who had believed, but he insisted that the Jewish people as a whole were a "holy lump" because of their election. He concluded from Romans 11:25ff. that they would be converted to Christ at the end of the age, "after the heathen, according to the fullness of the elect, have come in."

While Luther thus speaks in his commentary on Romans as one who believed in the final conversion of the Jews, he later changed his mind and came to accept the interpretation of Romans favored by many of the ancient Fathers of the church. In the end he assumed that when Paul spoke of the salvation of "all Israel" (11:26) and the coming in of the "full number of the Gentiles" (11:25) he was referring to one and the same event. In other words, Paul assumed that "all Israel" was the whole number of the elect, both Jew and Gentile, who would be brought to salvation through the preaching of the gospel from apostolic times until the judgment day.[5] This change in his understanding of Romans corresponds to his growing

---

4. Luther, *Commentary on the Epistle to the Romans*, trans. J. Theodore Mueller (Grand Rapids: Zondervan, 1954), p. 144.

5. See Mueller's comment in Luther's *Commentary on the Epistle to the Romans*, pp. 145 – 46.

intolerance of the Jews. Toward the end of his life, forgetting all that he had ever said about their election, he railed against the Jews as having "a devilish heart, hard as a block of wood, stone, and iron" ("*ein Herz stock-stein-eisen-teufelhart*") that could not be moved. He advised that they be expelled from Christian lands, that their books be banned, and that their synagogues be burned; and in a sermon he delivered shortly before he died, he warned that they were dangerous public enemies who ought not to be tolerated.[6]

Though Calvin never succumbed to the bitter invective of Luther, he understood Romans 9–11 much as Luther had toward the end of his life. According to such a view, the Jews as a people have no particular future in God's redemptive purpose. Rather, when Paul speaks of the "hardening . . . come upon part of Israel, until the full number of the Gentiles come in" (11:25), "Israel" is a reference to Jews as distinct from Gentiles, but when in the following verse (11:26) he says, "and so all Israel shall be saved," he means by "Israel" not Jews as such but *spiritual* Israel—that is, all the elect of God, both Jews and Gentiles. The assumption is that the whole body of God's people is called "Israel" because the Jews were the firstborn of God's family and therefore entitled to preeminence. Nevertheless, it is maintained that the kingdom of Christ is by no means confined to the Jews, but rather that it includes the whole world. Just how the Lord will gather to himself the faithful remnant among the Jews who are not hardened is, as Paul says, a "mystery" (11:25)—which is to say, it is incomprehensible until God shall reveal it to us through the unfolding of his providence. Thus Calvin speaks as though the salvation of the Jews were a future event, yet he seems not to contemplate their conversion in any large numbers even at the end of the age. He holds that the "until" ($\alpha\chi\rho\iota\varsigma\ o\upsilon$) of verse 25 does not signify an order of time; in fact, he translates the verse, "a partial blindness has come upon Israel (the Jews) that the full number of the Gentiles may come in."

This view, which was taken by the Reformers, has dominated the creeds and confessions coming out of the Protestant Reformation. It involves a subtle though not insignificant change in the self-understanding of the church vis-à-vis the Jews. The church no

---

6. See Philip Schaff, *History of the Christian Church*, 8 vols. (New York: Scribners, 1910), 8/2: 62. Shades of the Holocaust!

longer shares its status as God's chosen people with Israel. Rather, the church is the people of God in a way that excludes Israel, save for those few Jews who confess Christ and thereby cease to be Jews because they have become Christians. The election of the church, in other words, supersedes rather than supplements the election of Israel. There is no more an election of Israel, understanding the term "Israel" in the literal sense of the Jewish people, but only an election of the church.

As we have already noted, this traditional understanding of the way in which the church has inherited Israel's election is in fact anti-Semitic. The teaching that the church is elect, *not along with*, but *instead of* Israel, implies that God has in the end rejected the Jews as his people. And when this inference is drawn, it lends itself to the facile conclusion that the Jews have been repudiated by God for being guilty of the supreme sin of Deicide. In the matter of corporate election, the Jews are given the status of Judas in the matter of individual election. The extensive statement of Paul concerning Israel in the flesh (Rom. 9–11) is minimized, and the statement in 1 Thessalonians 2:14–16 that God's wrath has come upon the Jews is understood to mean that they are the subject of his wrath finally and forever. We shall return to this passage presently.

Since Pope John XXIII and the Second Vatican Council, the Roman Catholic Church has had a more open and positive view of the Jewish people. The Dogmatic Constitution *Lumen Gentium* (1964), speaking of the ways in which those who have not yet received the gospel are related to the people of God, asserts that the Jews stand in the first place as "a people of election most dear to God because of their Fathers; for the gifts and the call of God are irrevocable (cf. Rom. 9:4–5)."[7] The Protestant view of the place of Israel in God's purpose reflects a broad spectrum of theological opinion, from cultural assimilation into the (liberal) church on the one side to strict biblical literalism of a restored Jewish nation on the other. Sad to say, for all the efforts to achieve an improved theological stance, anti-Semitism is increasing in both Catholic and Protestant countries today.

---

7. See *Christian Faith: Doctrinal Documents in Catholic Faith*, ed. J. Neuner and J. Dupuis (Westminster, Md.: Christian Classics, 1975), p. 274.

2. Their Election Affirmed

Obviously there is something wrong with this view of matters. How different is the spirit in which Paul addresses the question of Israel and the church from that which has marked the Christian tradition through the centuries. He begins the discussion confessing his great sorrow and continued anguish for his brothers and sisters, his kindred according to the flesh (Rom. 9:2–3). Even if we were to discount this testimony as simply reflecting his personal situation—and surely we should not do so—what he goes on to say simply does not fit with the theory that the church has taken the place of Israel as God's chosen people. Convinced as he was that the church had inherited Israel's election and covenant, he nonetheless believed most ardently that God, who had grafted the wild branches into the good olive tree, would one day graft the original branches back on again (Rom. 11:17–24). Of this he was sure because the gifts and calling of God are irrevocable. It was Paul's understanding that Israel remains God's people, beloved for the sake of their forebears according to election (κατα δε την εκλογην αγαπητοι δια τους πατερας, Rom. 11:28–29).

In telling the Romans about the contribution that the churches of Macedonia and Achaia had made to relieve the poor among the saints of Jerusalem, Paul observes that they were indeed in debt to them, "for if the Gentiles have come to share in their spiritual blessings, they ought also to be of service to them in material blessings" (Rom. 15:26–27). We should take note of his use of the verb "to share": when it comes to things spiritual, sharing rather than supplanting is the key to understanding how the New Testament relates Israel to the church. In the mystery of God's saving purpose, the church does not dispossess Israel but rather shares their election and covenant with them. To say this is not to trivialize the solemn warning of our Lord that the kingdom would be taken from unbelieving Israel (Matt. 21:43), any more than it is to trivialize the vivid figure of Paul that the unbelieving branches have been broken off from the olive tree (Rom. 11:17–21). These passages, however, and others like them, speak a penultimate rather than an ultimate word concerning Israel; the ultimate word is that God has not rejected his people whom he foreknew—that is, whom he chose beforehand

(Rom. 11:2).[8] Hence, we must formulate our doctrine of corporate election — election and the people of God — so as to include rather than exclude Israel. Though there was once an Israel without the church, there never would have been a church had there been no Israel; and there never will be a church without Israel.[9] God's gifts and calling to Israel are irrevocable (Rom. 11:29).

3. Israel's Future and the Christian Vision

If it is true that the Christian understanding of Israel rests on the doctrine of election, an election that the church shares with Israel as the people of God, what is to be said of the long-standing antagonism that has divided Jews and Christians? How, if ever, can it finally be resolved? Much as we may hope to purge out the leaven of anti-Semitism from the Christian psyche, we must face the fact that Jews and Christians are divided in a profound way, in a way that essentially has nothing to do with anti-Semitism. It is rather a matter of the relationship of election to the covenant as the Christians (taught by Paul, himself a Jew) understand that relationship. According to the Christian view, election makes the covenant a matter of grace. Those who are in a covenant relationship with God are in this relationship because they are chosen by him apart from any merit of their own. Hence, the covenant cannot be understood in terms of law. The law, as Paul says, since it "came four hundred and thirty years afterward, does not annul a covenant previously ratified by God, so as to make the promise void" (Gal. 3:17).

But at the time the Christian church came into being, the Jewish people as a whole understood their covenant as a legal engagement. Hence, they made the keeping of the law the ground of divine favor. This is what the apostle had in mind when he described the Judaism of his day as "the present Jerusalem . . . in slavery with her children" (Gal. 4:25). Paul bore his people witness that they did indeed have a zeal for God, but not according to knowledge (Rom. 10:2). They were seeking, as he once did, to establish their own

---

8. It should be noted that "choose beforehand" is the meaning lexicographers give in this text and in Romans 8:29. See Bauer, *A Greek-English Lexicon of the New Testament and Other Early Christian Literature*, trans. W. F. Arndt and F. W. Gingrich, 4th ed. (Chicago: University of Chicago Press, 1957), p. 710.

9. On this, see Andre Lacocque, *But as for Me: The Question of Election in the Life of God's People Today* (Atlanta: John Knox, 1979), p. 21.

righteousness because they understood the covenant as requiring works rather than promising grace. And because they thus misconstrued the covenant, they rejected the righteousness that the covenant secures as a gift of God through faith in Christ—the Christ who is the end of the law for righteousness to all who believe (Rom. 10:2–4). To be sure, not all Jewish people have failed to obtain the blessing of the covenant: the elect, who like the faithful in Elijah's day are a remnant chosen by grace, have obtained it (Rom. 11:2–7). But the rest are hardened, and a veil lies over the eyes of their mind whenever they read the covenant, a veil that can be taken away only through Christ (2 Cor. 3:14–16).

In this context one can understand the severe indictment of 1 Thessalonians 2:14–16, in which the apostle accuses his brethren of killing both the Lord Jesus and the prophets and of driving him out and hindering him from speaking to the Gentiles that they might be saved. Having misunderstood the covenant, they failed to fulfill the mission for which they had been chosen and elected. Rather than becoming a blessing to all nations through the sharing of the gospel, they sought to prevent the apostles from even so much as speaking to the Gentiles about salvation. Thus they had filled up the measure of their sins and finally become the objects of divine wrath "in a most decisive way."[10]

But if this is not Paul's last word on the subject (and I would suggest that it is not), what is the future of God's chosen people, the Jews? The prophets of the Old Testament were the first to struggle with the question of whether Israel's election could remain valid if the covenant were not kept. There was always the dark possibility that Yahweh might reject Israel as he had the Ethiopians, Philistines, and Syrians (Amos 9:7). Yet the prophets dared to believe that though Israel become *Lo-ruhama* ("not pitied") and *Lo-ammi* ("not my people"), yet they would again be called "sons and daughters of the living God" (Hos. 1:6–11). Paul obviously shared this hope for his

---

10. Since the εις τελος of verse 16 admits of several meanings, one's interpretation of this text will depend on one's general theological position concerning the Jews. As we have noted, it seems impossible in the light of Paul's fuller statement in Romans 9–11 to suppose that he is here saying that the Jews have become the objects of God's wrath "to all eternity." Yet it is also clear that Paul believed the special privilege they enjoyed as the chosen people aggravated rather than ameliorated their offense. See also Matthew 23:29ff.

people, as we have already noted. However, he goes beyond the prophets in that he expresses this hope so as to include the Gentiles to whom the gospel of Christ has come.

The Jews have indeed stumbled in their present unbelief, but their fall is not in order that they might suffer irrevocable ruin (Rom. 11:11). The latter is unthinkable (μη γενοιτο)—because of their election: "As regards the gospel, they are enemies of God for [the Gentiles'] sake; but as regards their election, they are beloved for the sake of their forefathers" (Rom. 11:28). The mysterious purpose of God in Israel's present rejection is that by their rejection, salvation might come to the Gentiles.[11] And this salvation of the Gentiles, in turn, has as its purpose the salvation of the Jews: "Through their trespass salvation has come to the Gentiles, so as to make Israel jealous" (Rom. 11:11). So far as Israel and the Gentiles are concerned, there is a kind of undulating mutuality in their salvation. Israel was originally elected out of the Gentiles—"Your fathers lived of old beyond the Euphrates . . . and served other gods" (Josh. 24:2)—in order to bring salvation to the Gentiles—"by your descendants shall all the nations of the earth bless themselves" (Gen. 22:18). Now this purpose is being fulfilled, yet in a mysterious way. Through Israel's unbelief salvation has come to the Gentiles, and this salvation of the Gentiles shall lead in due course to the final salvation of Israel as well. "As God causes the salvation that has redounded from the wall of Israel's unbelief to stream out to the Gentiles," says H. N. Ridderbos, "so it must be his hidden intention therewith that the Gentiles become a cause of deliverance for Israel."[12]

Of course our understanding of the way in which Israel's rejection has led to the reconciliation of the Gentile world (Rom. 11:15) is clearer than our understanding of how the reconciliation

---

11. Paul and Barnabas, being thrust out of the synagogue in Pisidian Antioch, replied, "It was necessary that the word of God should be spoken first to you. Since you thrust it from you and judge yourselves unworthy of eternal life, behold, we turn to the Gentiles. . . . And when the Gentiles heard this, they were glad and glorified the word of God; and as many as were ordained to eternal life believed" (Acts 13:46, 48). This incident illustrates the pattern of Paul's Gentile mission as a whole. It also illumines his well-known manifesto that the gospel is "the power of God for salvation . . . to the Jew *first* and also to the Greek" (Rom. 1:16).

12. Ridderbos, *Paul: An Outline of His Theology* (Grand Rapids: William B. Eerdmans, 1975), p. 358.

of the Gentile world will ultimately mean the reconciliation of Israel. The former is remarkable—it has led to the "enrichment" of the Gentiles and, indeed, of the world (Rom. 11:12)—but the latter will be as "life from the dead" (Rom. 11:15). Paul sums up his thought in the following familiar words:

> I want you to understand this mystery, brethren: a hardening has come upon part of Israel, until the full number of the Gentiles come in, and so all Israel will be saved. . . . Just as you were once disobedient to God but now have received mercy because of their disobedience, so they have now been disobedient in order that by the mercy shown to you they also may receive mercy. For God has consigned all men to disobedience, that he may have mercy upon all. (Rom. 11:25–26, 30–32)

Though there are many interpretations of this difficult passage,[13] some things seem relatively clear.

1. Paul envisions the salvation of his people, assuming that their rejection is not total or final. Moreover, he envisions the same sort of salvation for his people that the Gentiles have come to know through his ministry as the apostle of Jesus Christ to the Gentiles: there is ultimately one elect people of God.

2. This salvation, so far as Israel is concerned, is to have a much fuller manifestation than anything the apostle had known in his day. It was for him, as it is for us, an event that would take place in the future.

3. The *crux interpretum* is Romans 11:25b–26a: "a hardening has come upon part of Israel, until the full number of the Gentiles come in, and so all Israel will be saved" (οτι πωρωσις απο μερους τω Ισραηλ γεγονεν αχρις ου το πληρωμα των εθνων εισελθη, και ουτως πας Ισραηλ σωθησεται).

Here the apostle clearly seems to say that there is a definite, if mysterious, interdependence between Israel and the Gentiles in the matter of salvation. At the time that the full number of Gentiles has "come in"—that is, "come in to the blessings of salvation"—Israel also shall be saved, shall enter into those same blessings. This salvation will mark the end of the partial hardening that presently

---

13. See G. Schrenk, "λειμμα," *Theological Dictionary of the New Testament*, 10 vols., ed. Gerhard Kittel and Gerhard Friedrich, trans. Geoffrey W. Bromiley [Grand Rapids: William B. Eerdmans, 1964–76], 4: 209–14.

accounts for their unbelief. When this happens, God's purpose in electing a people, both Jew and Gentile, will be fulfilled. Rather than speculate about when and how this divine purpose will be fulfilled (which the apostle does not do), we should join him in adoring the wisdom and knowledge that conceived such a purpose and confess that God's judgments are unsearchable and his ways past finding out (Rom. 11:33).

Many, however, have not been willing to leave unresolved the question of when and how Israel is to be saved. They have speculated that this future salvation of the Jewish people will come as a sudden national conversion at the end of the age, following the conversion of the Gentiles. A "nation" will be "born in a day." Says Charles Hodge,

> There were to be and have been numerous conversions to Christianity from among the Jews, in every age since the advent; but their *national* conversion is not to occur until the heathen are converted. . . . All that can be safely inferred from this language ["until the full number of the Gentiles come in"] is that the Gentiles as a body, the races of the Gentile world, will be converted before the restoration of the Jews as a nation.[14]

Behind this way of speaking is the thesis, common to the Reformed tradition, that prior to the coming of Christ, Israel was elect in a double sense: in an outward and temporal sense, the nation, as a nation, was elect; in an inward, personal, and eternal sense, a faithful remnant was elect. This latter election is presumed to continue as devout individuals from among the Jewish people turn to Christ in every age. The former (national) election is presumed to have ceased with the coming of Christ, who was rejected by the Jews as a whole. Still, Hodge reasons, there is a sense in which this former, national election will be renewed in the conversion of the Jewish people as a whole in the end time.

There is much to be said for this approach of an outer and inner election (an "Israel within Israel") as a means of resolving the problem of how Israel can be regarded as God's elect people even though the majority continue to reject Christ even to the present

---

14. Hodge, *Commentary on Romans* (Grand Rapids: William B. Eerdmans, 1955), pp. 373–74.

day. It becomes problematic, however, when one speaks of "Israel's salvation as a *nation* at the end of the age." Hodge, of course, was using the term loosely, for he knew nothing of the state of Israel back in 1886, when his commentary was first published. But now that there is such a political entity, it would seem best to refer to the future of Israel in terms of the salvation of God's *people* rather than of the *nation* of Israel as such.

In this regard, we might note that Paul says nothing one way or the other about the restoration of Israel as a national state in the land occupied by the Old Testament tribes. He was neither a Zionist nor an anti-Zionist, but a Jew who had become a Christian. When he thought of his fellow Jews, he thought of them as the people of God, regardless of whether they lived in the homeland that had become the Roman province of Judea or whether they lived in the diaspora. He was not concerned with their *national* status but with their *theological* status as elect and chosen by God. His concern was not with their restoration to Palestine but with their restoration to the blessings of the covenant through salvation in Christ. He had hoped to realize such a response through his preaching; though it proved to be a hope unfulfilled, it remained a hope unshaken—and so it remains down to the present for all Christians who earnestly pray for the peace of Jerusalem.

Addendum
A Parenthetical Remark on Dispensationalism

At this point a brief word is in order concerning a distinctive approach to the question of Israel's future that takes a rather different tack, stressing not the mutuality of Israel and the church as the elect people of God but rather their duality. In the school of thought known in American theological circles as Dispensationalism, popularized in the *Scofield Reference Bible*, the distinction between Israel and the church is sharply drawn. As C. C. Ryrie puts it,

> The essence of dispensationalism . . . is the distinction between Israel and the church. This grows out of the dispensationalist's consistent employment of normal or plain interpretation [of Scripture, specifically Old Testament prophecy] and it reflects a basic understanding of the purpose of God in all his dealing with mankind as that of glorifying himself through salvation and other purposes as well.[15]

L. S. Chafer presses this radical distinction between Israel and the church back into the eternal counsel of God. God is pursuing two distinct purposes, Chafer contends — one relating to his earthly people, the Jews, and the other to his heavenly people, the church. Hence, these two have eternally different destinies: the former shall dwell forever on a glorified earth; the latter, in a glorious heaven.

Because Dispensationalists take Old Testament prophecy in this "literal," "plain," "normal" sense, the future restoration of the Jewish people to their ancestral land — of which the New Testament says nothing — makes the events surrounding the state of Israel a key to understanding everything else that is happening in our world today. (Hal Lindsey's Dispensationalist treatise *The Late Great Planet Earth* has been vastly popular, garnering sales in the millions.) This seemingly straightforward, literal interpretation of prophecy also explains the insistence among Dispensationalists that when Christ returns he will reign literally on the throne of his father David for a

---

15. Ryrie, *Dispensationalism Today* (Chicago: Moody, 1965), p. 47.

thousand years. According to those who take Ezekiel 40–48 literally, the temple and blood sacrifice will also be restored during this millennial reign. (And indeed, if prophecy is to be taken literally, then it should be taken literally.)

Not only are there theological problems with Dispensationalism—such as the fact that it turns the redemptive clock back to Old Testament blood sacrifice—but there are possible ethical problems as well. In a recent "Declaration" signed by prominent Dispensationalists and others, the following points were affirmed:

> 1. All of the Holy Land is the inalienable possession of the Jewish People, . . . and the establishment of modern Israel is an undeniable fulfillment of Biblical prophecy, the herald of the coming Messiah.
>
> 2. Jerusalem is the eternal and indivisible capital of the Jewish State.
>
> 3. Israel should not be required to cede disputed land in return for "peace"—a peace which is her legitimate birthright; that much of that disputed land falls within her biblically mandated borders, and that a fair and unbiased application of accepted international justice may well permit Israel the option of retaining the disputed territories.[16]

Needless to say, few theologians—myself included—have found this view of God's electing purpose for Israel particularly helpful, and so we have not pursued such an approach in our efforts to understand Israel's relation to the church as the elect people of God.

---

16. See the Declaration issued by the participants in the "Evangelical-Christian and Jewish Leadership Encounter," Washington, D.C., 11 November 1982.

4

Election and the Individual

As we have seen in the previous section, in the Bible the elect are generally spoken of as a class, not as individuals per se. Yet the implication is plain, especially in the New Testament, that each member who belongs to the fellowship of the elect shares, as an individual, in the election of that people. The doctrine of election, in other words, has not only a corporate but also an individual aspect. The elect are not only all those together whom God has chosen to be the objects of his grace and favor, but each one in particular.[1] As we are saved in and for fellowship (the church), so we are chosen of God to be his people, yet as individuals. God's love, as Dorothy Sayers reminds us,

> is anxiously directed to confirm each individual soul in its own identity, so that, the nearer it draws to Him, the more truly it becomes its unique and personal self. . . . The Infinite came once into the finite as a single and particular Person; the company of His elect is made up of single and particular persons. . . . If we try to efface from the Christian revelation the brand of singularity, then what we shall have left is not Christianity at all.[2]

---

1. When used to describe a specific individual, the adjective *elect* most likely means "preeminent," "of excellent qualities," as the "elect lady" to whom John sends greetings from the children of her "elect sister" (2 John 13). When used of Jesus individually, it designates him as chosen to the office of Messiah (Luke 9:35; 23:35).

2. Sayers, Introduction to vol. 2 of Dante's *The Divine Comedy*, trans. Dorothy Sayers, 3 vols. (Harmondsworth: Penguin, 1959), 2: 37.

Because God's electing love is love for the individual *as* an individual, we know that it is personal and intimate. As the oriental shepherd called his sheep by name, so Jesus as the good Shepherd "knows" his sheep (John 10:14). This individual quality in God's electing love is reflected in the use of the singular personal pronoun in Scripture: He loved *me* and gave himself for *me* (Gal. 2:20). To be elect is to be aware that God has fixed his love on *me*, called *me* by my name, given *me* a new name (Rev. 2:17), and inscribed *my* name in his Book.[3] To be a Christian, then, is to be one of God's elect and thus an heir of eternal salvation.[4]

It is especially in the New Testament that the individual aspect of election becomes prominent, and it is largely in terms of individual election that the doctrine has been discussed by theologians.[5] This seeming imbalance in the theological discussion is the result, at least in part, of the many seemingly intractable problems that attach to the doctrine as it relates to the individual. Before we review these problems and the solutions that have traditionally been proffered, we should pause to summarize and comment on the unique way in which Barth approaches this most difficult of questions.

A SUMMARY OF BARTH'S VIEW

Barth gives the individual aspect of election a unique turn in his *Dogmatics*. In a remarkable passage, he construes the history of Israel as an ever-narrowing set of concentric circles with Jesus Christ at the center. He grants that there is, of course, expansion from Abraham, Isaac, and Jacob to the twelve patriarchs and finally to the nation Israel, but he contends that this unique community, a humanity within humanity, is cut back (as symbolized from the

---

3. One can only deplore the pedanticism of hymnbook editors and "liturgical experts" who alter singular personal pronouns to the plural for congregational use: "When *we* survey the wondrous cross . . . ."

4. Though election is unto salvation, its purpose is sometimes more specifically given, as when Jesus tells his disciples that he has chosen (elected, εξελεξαμην) them out of the world that they should bear fruit in the world (John 15:16, 19).

5. The fact that Romans 9–11 remains the *locus classicus* whether one is concerned with election as corporate or individual presents a clear indication that we should make neither too much nor too little of the emphasis on the individual in the New Testament.

beginning by the rejection of Ishmael and Esau) until Israel, separated out of the whole human race, becomes Judah, and Judah, carried away into exile, becomes a mere remnant. This remnant returns to prepare the coming of him who is great David's greater Son, that single Individual, Jesus Christ, the electing God who is the elected Man (CD, 2/2: 51–58).

In the elaboration and defense of this thesis, Barth argues that Jesus Christ cannot be elect as human only, for then he would not have the authority to be Lord and Head of all the elect (CD, 2/2: 94–194). He then would be only the object, not the Subject, of election. Hence, we must assume that his being elected as a creature presupposes his electing act as the Creator. When we read in Ephesians 1:4 that all others are chosen (elect) "in him," this does not mean simply that they are elect "with" him and "through" him, says Barth, but rather "in His person, in His will, in His own divine choice" (CD, 2/2: 117). As the elect human he, in his humanity, is the One who is at the same time the God who elects all.

Only when we have said this can we go on to say that his election is exemplary of ours (the "mirror of our election," as Calvin puts it), that his election is the instrument and organ of ours. (Barth approves, in this revised sense, the Arminian formula used at Dort — namely, that Christ is the "foundation of election"; although it was rightly rejected by the Synod, he contends that the Arminians originally meant it simply in the sense that Christ is the basis of the offer of salvation, an offer one may accept or reject.)

By identifying the elect Human Being as the electing God, Barth claims to be returning to the Christological principle that had strangely been abandoned in favor of the traditional tendency to think of the elective decree as the act of the Father rather than of the Son. The Son, he suggests, is wrongly understood to come not as the One who *chooses* but as the One who *is chosen* by his Father for his messianic task. He argues that such a view implies that the Son, who became incarnate as the Christ, is simply the first elect human and that we are elected "for him," not "in him." This would make him the foundation of our *salvation* but not of our *election* and thus rob us of the comfort of our salvation inasmuch as we would have no recourse from the choice behind him, a choice hidden in the counsels of eternity.

To put the problem another way, although I am rightly told

to look to Christ for my salvation, the traditional view implies that my salvation ultimately depends not on him to whom I look but on the Father, whose eternal decision concerning me (election) is one of which I can never be sure in this life. But if election is the act of the Word who became flesh, who is then acted upon (elected), and we in him, then in election we have to do not with Calvin's hidden God (*Deus nudus absconditus*) but with the revealed God (*Deus revelatus*) in Jesus Christ. And if this is the God with whom we have to do, argues Barth, there can be no hidden God whose eternal purpose negates his revealed purpose. Thus, we are assured that his revealed will corresponds to his eternal will. It is the God who reveals himself as reconciled to the world through the death of his Son (2 Cor. 5:19) who is the electing God. Barth expresses his puzzlement that no one ever thought of all this before, since he maintains that it enables us to escape the mystery first of God's hidden will and second of his choosing an unknown number of people according to that will.

We get a clearer picture of just how Barth would escape this twofold mystery when we turn to the question of *double* predestination. It has commonly been assumed that election implies reprobation. Barth would not deny that this is so; he is himself a double predestinarian. But he holds that those who espouse this double predestination — predestination to life (election) and to death (reprobation) — have typically missed a decisive insight concerning the *object* of predestination: they have assumed that God has irrevocably chosen a fixed number of elect individuals on the one hand and reprobate on the other — a number fixed from all eternity in his hidden counsel.[6]

But, Barth insists, God in Christ is revealed as the God who himself elects and so is elected to suffer in the sinner's place. Thus, Jesus Christ as the Elect becomes the one true Reprobate. He is the individual Human Being whose election is the eternal decision that he shall take the sinner's No to himself. He is, in the words of the apostle, "made sin for us." And this he does in order that the human

---

6. Such has indeed been the traditional assumption: "These angels and men, thus predestined and foreordained, are particularly and unchangeably designed; and their number is so certain and definite that it cannot be either increased or diminished," Westminster Confession, chap. 3, sect. 4.

No of sin may lose its authority in the divine Yes whereby in him we become the righteousness of God (2 Cor. 5:21). Because of the eternal decision that he shall suffer the divine wrath, judgment is pronounced and punishment is inflicted on him as the Rejected One. Thus predestination, precisely because it is double predestination, is good news. It is the beginning of the gospel that evokes in the sinner only joy and gratitude.

To anyone who has contemplated the problems besetting the doctrine of election, Barth's effort is arresting, to say the least. There is no denying that it resolves some of the most recalcitrant problems in the traditional view. But it is also clearly the case that it is beset with its own problems. For one thing, while it is true that the works of God *ad extra* are one and thus that election is the decision and choice of the one God—Father, Son, and Spirit—it nevertheless remains the case that election is also *per appropriationem* the work of the Father. Theologians have spoken this way because the Scriptures speak this way: the Scriptures bless the "God and Father of our Lord Jesus Christ . . . who chose us in him before the foundation of the world" (Eph. 1:3–4).

The Subject of election, then, is just God, or God the Father. The Scriptures never speak of Jesus Christ as the electing God. Rather, he is the one Mediator between God and humankind (1 Tim. 2:5), in the divine actions both of creation and of salvation. As all things are made *through* him ($\delta\iota'$ $\alpha\upsilon\tau\sigma\upsilon$, John 1:3), so all the elect are chosen *in* him ($\epsilon\nu$ $\alpha\upsilon\tau\omega$, Eph. 1:4).

Moreover, to solve the problem of double predestination as Barth does is to take more than a furtive glance in the direction of universalism. Brunner pointedly asks,

> But what does this statement, "that Jesus is the only really rejected man" mean for the situation of Man? Evidently this, that there is no such thing as being "lost," that there is no possibility of condemnation, and thus that there is no final Divine Judgment. Karl Barth has been charged with teaching Universalism. When he denies this he is not altogether wrong. He knows too much about the not particularly illustrious theologians who have taught this doctrine of *Apokatastasis* in Christian history to be willing to allow himself to be numbered among them. "The Church ought not to preach Apokatastasis." Thus Barth's doctrine is not that of Origen and his followers.
>
> Rather, Barth goes much further . . . [suggesting that] since

Jesus Christ appeared, and through Him, there are no longer any who are rejected. Not only for those who are "in Him" through faith, but for all men, hell has been blotted out, condemnation and judgment eliminated. This is not a deduction which I have drawn from Barth's statement, but it is his own. Since Jesus Christ has taken the condemnation of sin upon Himself "rejection cannot again become the portion of man." . . . "Even the rejected stand in this light of Election."[7]

Brunner goes on to observe that the implication of Barth's doctrine of election contradicts the plain teaching of the New Testament that "whoever believes in him should not perish," but that "he who does not believe is condemned already" (John 3:16, 18).

There is, in my judgment, ample basis for Brunner's complaint. Whereas the traditional doctrine of election has regarded the divine choice as primary and the human choice as secondary, Barth's doctrine tends to make the divine choice not simply the primary but the *only* choice. Hence, he speaks of the difference between the believer and the unbeliever as a "relative" difference: the elect know their solidarity with the godless, whose unbelief is the only thing that separates them. Unbelievers are rejected in a secondary but not in an ultimate sense. They can never bring down on their head the same sword of the divine wrath a second time, now that it has decisively fallen on Jesus Christ. Because Jesus Christ is both *the* Elect and *the* Rejected, both the elect and the rejected exist "in him" and he is the Lord and Head of both. The two groups stand alongside each other and *over against* him, and so on (see *CD*, 2/2: 340–409). As Brunner puts it, in Barth's theology the lost only appear to be lost; they are like sailors in a storm on a shallow pond.

Nowhere is this problem more evident than in the section in which Barth deals with the lost specifically. Even the title of the subsection, "The Determination of the Rejected" (*CD*, 2/2: 449–506), should serve to alert the discerning reader. It speaks of "the Rejected" (*Verworfenen*)—the *objects* of God's rejection—whereas the argument that follows is concerned with those who say No to Christ, with *subjects* who act to "reject" their "election." In other

---

7. Brunner, *Dogmatics*, vol. 1, *The Christian Doctrine of God*, trans. Olive Wyon, Lutterworth Library, vol. 35 (London: Lutterworth Press, 1949), pp. 348–49.

words, although Barth is talking about the reject*ing* ones, he is compelled to speak of them as the reject*ed* ones. Why is this? Because they are the counterpart of the elect of whom he speaks in the previous paragraph, and he describes them as the elect*ed* ones, the *objects* of God's electing grace. The elect are not the subjects of their own election; they do not elect themselves. But the "rejected" *are*, according to Barth, the subject of their own rejection. Though they are elected (for all are elect in Christ), they reject their election. In a very elemental way, this proposition simply does not make sense. How can the one who is elected in Christ (by God) be rejected in himself (by God)?

In an effort to solve this riddle, Barth engages in a long discussion in which he seeks to ameliorate the solemn "woe" Jesus pronounced upon Judas in anticipation of his betrayal (see Mark 14:21 par.). The attempt amounts to fifty pages of fine print that can only be described as an exercise in quixotic theologizing—if we might add a new theology to the list. Barth points to Judas as the primary paradigm of the rejected. Here we have the problem of an irresistible divine grace from above meeting an immovable human resistance from below. Barth reminds us that as we turn to this case, we must not forget that Judas was one of the twelve and therefore just as much chosen and elect as the rest. Furthermore, he contends, the Son of Man had to be handed over by someone if he were to accomplish his task as the Rejected One. He suggests Judas's treachery, heinous though it was, relates to Peter's denial as Saul's ritual offense relates to David's adultery! With Judas, as is so often the case, the sin of the rejected seems less significant than the sin of the elected. Can his sin, then, latent in all of the apostles ("Lord, is it I?"), nullify the meaning of Christ's death on his behalf?

After discussing the Matthias episode (Acts 2:23–26), Barth decides that Paul, not Matthias, is Judas's real successor. And since Paul takes Judas's place, Judas "in his own place and after his own fashion [is] *the* outstanding apostle" (*CD*, 2/2: 479). He had a proximity to Jesus in death that none of the others knew, says Barth: as the one who handed Jesus over, Judas stood beside Jesus in the death that witnessed to his rejection, a death he suffered in order to bear away our rejection. Similarly, as the one who encountered the risen Lord on the Damascus road, Paul stood beside Jesus in the resurrection that witnessed to his divine election to life, an election that answers to our election. Barth ruminates on the fact that the same word (παραδοσις) is used to describe Judas's act of betrayal and Paul's delivery of the gospel (CD, 2/2: 481). As Judas the "negative apostle" delivers over Jesus to the rulers, so Paul the "positive apostle" delivers him over to his hearers in the kerygma, thus rectifying the havoc wrought by his "predecessor."

And so, says Barth, we may dare to see at least a secondary reversal of Judas's rejection in his positive counterpart Paul, a type as it were of the primary eschatological reversal implied in the fact that long before Judas delivered up Jesus, God delivered him up — he is the "Lamb slain from before the foundation of the world" (Rev. 13:8) — for the salvation of all, including Judas. So while we cannot be dogmatic about what will happen to the rejected ones, he concludes, surely the bounds of their hell are limited by the greater hell that our Lord suffered for them that they might be delivered.

ELECTION AND JESUS CHRIST

Whatever reservations one may have about the conclusions to which Barth comes in the matter, there can be no doubt that Jesus' election is an important aspect of the doctrine in general. The Scriptures say little about the subject in an express way, but what they do say is of prime importance regarding the office and task to which he is chosen. As the king of Israel was the Lord's chosen (1 Sam. 10:24), so Jesus is chosen as God's Messiah, the Christ. This is the common confession of Christians. From the beginning they have seen Jesus as the Servant of the Lord referred to in Isaiah: "Behold my servant . . . my chosen, in whom my soul delights; I have put my spirit upon him, he will bring forth justice to the nations" (Isa. 42:1; cf. Matt. 12:18). In the Lucan account of the transfiguration, the Voice out of the theophanic cloud testifies, "This is my Son, my Chosen" (literally, the Elect One, ο εκλελεγμενος, Luke 9:35). Hence, Jesus is called the Christ — that is, the Anointed — "because he is ordained [chosen, elected] of God the Father, and anointed with the Holy Spirit, to be our chief Prophet and Teacher; our High Priest . . . and our eternal King" (Heidelberg Catechism, Q. 31).

Since Jesus is elected to be the Christ that he might save us from our sins, the issue that has concerned the theologians is how his election is related to ours. Augustine observed long ago that as one man was predestined to be our Head, so we, being many, are

ELECTION AND THE INDIVIDUAL

predestined to be his members. This intimate union between Christ and the elect has led the majority of theologians to the conclusion that Christ and his people share a common election. Though some (especially Lutherans) have been reluctant to embrace the thought that Christ is elect with us on the grounds that our election is from sin to salvation, others (especially among the Reformed) have argued that Christ is indeed the object of election together with his church despite this difference.[8]

Though it is true that our election involves deliverance from sin, we are delivered in order that we may enjoy everlasting life with Christ. It is not what we are *delivered from* but what we are *elected to* that is the element common to the election of Christ and his people. As we are elected to life, so is Christ our Lord, who triumphed over death in the resurrection. Yet there is obviously a difference between the Head and the members of the body in this respect as in all others. We are elect as living stones, but Christ is elect and precious as the chief Cornerstone (1 Pet. 2:4ff.). In other words, we are chosen in him, not he in us. But this Pauline phrase "in Christ" (εν Χριστω) has such a broad connotation—we are called (Phil. 3:14), justified (Rom. 8:1), sanctified (1 Cor. 1:2), and even die ("fall asleep") "in him" (1 Cor. 15:22)—that one may still ask what precisely it means to say that we are elect in Christ.

Obviously the phrase "in Christ" conveys the thought of an intimate union with him. But probing beyond this obvious meaning, theologians have found it difficult to agree on the specific nature of our union with Christ in election. Of many suggestions, the one that is perhaps most widely urged is that Christ's election is the basis (*fundamentum*) of our election. We are not elect in and of ourselves but only as we are given him by his Father. It is because the Father loved the Son from before the foundation of the world and bestowed on him a people as the reward of his messianic obedience (John 17:2, 6, 24) that we are elect. We are chosen, therefore, not on the basis of *our* merit, but of *his* as the obedient Servant of the Lord. This view has frequently been given a pastoral turn in order to

---

8. Obviously, that aspect of Barth's approach summarized in the preceding section is grounded in this tradition. To the objection that Christ cannot be elect, since election is from sin to salvation, the Reformed sometimes answer that angels, apart from sin, are said to be elect (1 Tim. 5:21). "By the decree of God, for the manifestation of his glory, some men *and angels* are predestined unto everlasting life" (Westminster Confession, chap. 3, sect. 3).

relieve the anxiety of those who question their election. In an oft-quoted passage in the *Institutes* Calvin comments,

> Those God has adopted as his sons are said to have been chosen not in themselves but in his Christ; for unless he could love them in him, he could not honor them with the inheritance of his Kingdom if they had not previously become partakers of him. But if we have been chosen in him, we shall not find assurance of our election in ourselves; and not even in God the Father, if we conceive him as severed from his Son. Christ, then, is the mirror wherein we must, and without self-deception may, contemplate our own election. For since it is into his body the Father has destined those to be engrafted whom he has willed from eternity to be his own, that he may hold as sons all whom he acknowledges to be among his members, we have a sufficiently clear and firm testimony that we have been inscribed in the book of life if we are in communion with Christ. (*Inst.*, 2, 24, 5)

As Calvin speaks of Christ as the mirror of election (*speculum electionis*), so Luther calls him the Book of Life (*librum vitae*).[9] Both expressions suggest that when we receive Christ, our faith brings the assurance that we are elect. Knowing that Christ has been chosen as our Prophet, Priest, and King, we know that we have been chosen as the beneficiaries of his saving work. In other words, his election is the guarantee of ours, and so our election is no longer a mystery hidden in God's secret counsel until the final judgment day: the Book of Life has been opened to us and we have seen our names written there. As the Heidelberg Catechism says, Christ has been ordained as our chief prophet that he might "*fully reveal* to us the secret counsel and will of God concerning our redemption" (Q. 31). Therefore there can be no other will of God apart from that proclaimed in Christ, no secret counsel that has not been revealed in him. Hence, there is no reason for me to ask whether I am elect: the anxiety that might evoke such a question is dispelled when I look away from myself to him in whose election I see myself elect. Christ's election, in other words, assures me of my election.

---

9. Cf. The Formula of Concord, Art. 11, sect. 12: "So far, therefore, may a godly person proceed with safety in meditation upon the article of the eternal election of God, even as far, that is, as is revealed in the Word of God. For the Word of God proposes to us Christ, the Book of Life, which through the preaching of the Gospel is opened and spread out before us, as it is written (Rom. 8:30): 'Whom he did predestinate, them he also called.' "

Addendum
Concerning Assurance and the Syllogismus Practicus

Preaching at St. Paul's Cathedral on the evening of Christmas Day, 1624, John Donne observed, "If I should inquire upon what occasion God elected me, and wrote my name in the Book of Life, I would sooner be afraid that it were not so than find a reason why it should be so."[10]

This fear that one's name is not written in the Book of Life has been an ongoing concern of theologians as they have endeavored in theoretical ways, but especially in practical ways, to state the doctrine of election so as to relieve the tremulous spirit. (In this regard Protestant thought differs from traditional Roman Catholic thought, in which the effort to determine that one is "assuredly in the number of the predestinate" is deemed presumptuous.)[11] At the heart of this effort is the problem of the so-called "practical syllogism" (*syllogismus practicus*). Of course the discussion concerning the assurance of one's election is not generally stated in such a formal way; the expression "practical syllogism" is simply a manner of speaking.[12] But to bring the discussion into focus one might use a syllogistic form such as the following:

> If those chosen in Christ are chosen in order that they might be holy and without blame before him in love (Eph. 1:4), and
>
> If I see in my life the fruits of such holiness and blamelessness,
>
> Then I may be assured that I am among those chosen in Christ.

---

10. Donne, in *Sermons of John Donne*, ed. T. Gill (New York: Meridian Books, 1958), p. 94.

11. See the Council of Trent's "Decree on Justification," chap. 12.

12. The term *syllogism* is qualified by the adjective *practical* to indicate that it has to do with truth lived out in the life of faith rather than with the abstract truth of reason. (One is reminded of the Kantian distinction between the "practical" and the "theoretical" reason.) The qualifying adjective, however, is hardly enough to overcome the rational overtones of the word *syllogism*; hence the usage must be deemed unfortunate, insofar as it echoes the Aristotelian methodology of Protestant Scholasticism. The unfortunate usage, however, does not impugn the substantive nature of the problem to which the syllogism is addressed.

This particular statement of the argument is open to the criticism that the minor premise grounds one's assurance in oneself rather than in Christ. By self-examination, empirical evidence, as it were, is gathered alongside and independent of the promise in Christ. This is the ground of the reservations Barth and others have felt concerning the statement made at Dort:

> The elect, in due time, . . . attain assurance of their eternal and unchangeable election, not by inquisitively prying into the secret and deep things of God [Barth would of course agree with this] but by observing in themselves with a splendid joy and holy pleasure, the infallible fruits of election pointed out in the word of God; such as a true faith in Christ, filial fear, a godly sorrow for sin, a hungering and thirsting after righteousness, etc.[13]

The trouble is that when we observe our faith, we have to pray the prayer, "Help my unbelief"; when we observe our fear and godly sorrow, we must confess that even our repentance needs repenting of. As Calvin reminds us in another place, were we to look to our own works, we could as easily deduce God's rejection as his election of us. He then quotes the beautiful sentiment of Augustine which points toward the resolution of the problem:

> "I do not say to the Lord, 'Despise not the works of *my* hands.' . . . I commend not the works of my hands, for I fear lest, when Thou lookest upon them, thou mayest find more sins than merit. This only I say, this I ask, this I desire: despise not the works of thy hands; see in me thy work, not mine. For if thou seest mine, thou wilt condemn it. If thou seest thine own, thou wilt crown it. For whatever good works are mine are from thee." (*Inst.*, 3, 14, 20)

The crucial question that an appeal to the syllogism raises is how we can look wholly to Christ for the assurance of our election and at the same time to ourselves (i.e., to our works) for a confirmation of that election. The resolution of this dilemma, theologically speaking, is achieved by moving from a Christological basis in

---

13. Canons of Dort, First Head of Doctrine, Of Divine Predestination, Art. 12, as translated in Schaff, *The Evangelical Protestant Creeds*, vol. 3 of *Bibliotheca symbolica ecclesiae universalis* (New York: Harper, 1877), pp. 583–84.

the major premise to a pneumatological basis in the minor premise.[14] As it is God the Father who chooses us in Christ his Son, so it is God the Spirit who conforms us to the image of the Son (Rom. 8:29) as he bears witness with our spirit that we are the children of God (Rom. 8:16). Thus we can affirm that "All who keep his commandments abide in him, and he in them. And by this we know that he abides in us, by the Spirit which he has given us" (1 John 3:24). When our assurance rests not only on God's work *for* us but also on his work *in* us, then we can say, in the words of the Thirty-Nine Articles of the Church of England, that

> the consideration of . . . our election in Christ is full of sweet, pleasant and unspeakable comfort to godly persons, and such as feel in themselves the working of the Spirit of Christ, mortifying the works of the flesh and their earthly members, and drawing up their mind to high and heavenly things, as well because it does greatly establish and confirm their faith of eternal salvation to be enjoyed through Christ, as because it does frequently kindle their love towards God. (Art. 17)[15]

This note of "sweet, pleasant and unspeakable comfort" is the note struck in Scripture concerning the Book of Life. It is not some *secret* list of names, the very thought of which agitates the devout, but a source of joy and gladness.[16] "Do not rejoice in this," says Jesus to his disciples, "that the spirits are subject to you; but rejoice that your names are written in heaven" (Luke 10:20). And Paul, speaking of Clement and the rest of his fellow workers as those whose

---

14. On this point I am especially indebted to G. C. Berkouwer (see his *Divine Election*, trans. Hugo Becker, Studies in Dogmatics [Grand Rapids: William B. Eerdmans, 1960], pp. 291ff.). The difficulty with the traditional statement of the syllogism as I have framed it is that it moves from a Christological major premise (God has chosen us in Christ unto holiness) to an anthropological minor premise (I see in my life the fruits of holiness). Thus a subtle form of self-justification threatens the argument.

15. As we have already noted, Wesley omitted this article on "Predestination and Election" altogether in the revision of the Thirty-Nine Articles for his followers. Though he was an ordained priest in the Church of England, he saw no such benefits stemming from a consideration of election. Those who profess to believe the doctrine, he insisted, must confess that often there is the return of doubts and fears (see his sermon "Free Grace").

16. Even when Scripture speaks of those whose names are not written in the Book of Life, it is no secret as to who they are: they are those who worship the beast (Rev. 13:8).

names are in the Book of Life, goes on to admonish his readers, "Rejoice in the Lord always; again I will say, Rejoice" (Phil. 4:4).[17]

It is as we rejoice, not in the good works we have achieved but in the Lord who has begun his good work in us (Phil. 1:6), that we have the comfort of our election. Our good works are the sign of our election, but the *foundation* is Jesus Christ in whom we are elect. And by his Spirit we are assured that we have passed from death to life, in that we love our brothers and sisters (1 John 3:14). While it is true that we are enjoined to give diligence to make our calling and election sure (2 Pet. 1:10), yet this imperative must be dialectically related to the indicative of the Spirit's witness. Without the imperative, the indicative might well lead to the presumption denounced by Trent; but without the indicative, the imperative would surely lead to the sort of disquieting doubts that can destroy the peace of conscience and make shipwreck of faith. As Schlatter has observed, the assurance that we are elect frees us from the anxious quest for support in ourselves, frees us from the need for self-justification, frees us for joy in all our action, since our relationship to God is secure. On the other hand, Schlatter insists, such assurance is not unrelated to our experience. The fact that divine election is first in the "order of salvation" does not mean that it is the first doctrine believed. We do not heed the call of the gospel because we are assured of our election. Rather, in the temporal event of calling, the otherwise inaccessible mystery of election is revealed. "Hence it is false to speak of our election before we have experienced the call of Christ. Only when we have learned obedience *to* him, are we ready to affirm our election *in* him."[18]

---

17. The thought that God has written our names in his Book gives comfort and solace in danger and assures us that our salvation does not depend on our own effort and merit but on his grace. This assurance is graciously given as we respond to the call of the gospel. Note Bunyan's reference in *The Pilgrim's Progress, passim*, to Christian's "little roll" which he kept "in his bosom."

18. A. Schlatter, *Das christliche Dogma* (Stuttgart: Calwer, 1923), p. 476; for Schlatter's general discussion of election, see pp. 474ff.

Barth also, for all his zeal to give assurance a Christological rather than an anthropological basis, rejects neither the syllogism nor the inclusion in it of the experiential:

> While his [the elect individual's] witness in and by itself does not give the slightest assurance, he cannot receive the witness of Jesus Christ and the Holy Spirit—which gives real assurance—unless he receives it from himself, unless he himself gives it in his faith and life and "works." It is as I

EFFORTS AT UNDERSTANDING

When one seeks to resolve the problem of election and the individual, one obviously places oneself between the Scylla of divine sovereignty and the Charybdis of human freedom. One must speak of the hiddenness of God in his revelation, of an event in time that is laden with eternity, of a human choice that reflects a prior divine choice. But how? How does one acknowledge a freedom that is truly divine without making the creature a mere puppet on the string of a tyrant? How does one preserve a freedom that is truly human without making the creature the final arbiter of his or her own destiny, which is the first lie of the serpent in the garden? How does one give meaning to temporal events if they are fixed in an eternal purpose, or conceive of a purpose that is supposedly infallible yet realized in and through historical contingencies? How can one talk of a revelation that is hidden without losing oneself in the labyrinthine speculations of the human mind, or affirm a hiddenness that is revealed without confining revelation within the narrow clarities of a human system?

The problems alluded to in these questions are both theoretical and practical. On the theoretical side, efforts to resolve the problem have led theologians to adopt significantly different methodologies; in short, they have found the doctrine of predestination to be the tail that wags the dog. Meanwhile, on the practical side, the controversies these efforts have engendered are without precedent, if not in intensity, yet surely in longevity.[19] Herder was thankful that the

---

live as an elect man that I am and shall be assured of my election. (CD, 2/2: 335)

Barth, of course, faults the traditional use of the syllogism in that those who appeal to it are typically concerned only with the practical question of our knowledge (assurance) of our election. They should recognize that this knowledge is not simply a practical matter, he contends, since the basis of our knowledge of election is the basis of our election — namely, Jesus Christ, not some hidden decree behind Christ. To appeal to a hidden decree of salvation rather than to the historical work of the Savior is to make that work a mere means of accomplishing what was decided antecedently and thus independently. This is not the true Reformed position, according to Barth, since Christ is the Origin, not simply the Executor, of our election.

19. Some scholars have theorized that Romans 9 itself reflects notes drawn from Paul's controversies with his Jewish opponents: "You will say to me then. . . ." "But who are you, a man, to answer . . . ?" (v. 20).

debate concerning the doctrine of grace had finally been resolved and exclaimed, "Wither the hand that ever raises it thence."[20] Then came Barth, who wrote over five hundred pages in the *Dogmatics* on election, thus adding new impetus to an old argument.[21]

Of course controversy is the stuff of which great theology is made. As soon as the controversies in the ancient church over God and Christ began to subside (Nicaea and Chalcedon), the controversy over sin and salvation inevitably arose. At the heart of that controversy was the question of whether salvation is a divine or a human work. (The fact that it is, in its way, a divine/human work— for the sinner is not a stock or stone—should not divert us from the *essential* issue.) It is no accident that this profound question engaged the energies of no less a theologian than Augustine; his rediscovery of the Pauline doctrine of grace, for all the controversy, has put the church forever in his debt. But there is something about this particular controversy that is troublesome. While the premier theologians (who work seriously with Scripture) are pretty much on one side, many reputable theologians, and many more sincere Christians, are on the other.

Having touched upon the main lines of the dispute in the historical summary, we need not go back over such points as the sharp controversy that the doctrine has generated even within the Calvinistic tradition itself (for more on that, see, for example, Harry Boer, *The Doctrine of Reprobation in the Christian Reformed Church* [Grand Rapids: Eerdmans, 1983]). Often, those who believe in the doctrine themselves simply steer clear of it, especially in the pulpit, as "too controversial," thereby emulating many of the ancient theologians who applied a kind of "shunning" rule to the conclusions of Augustine on grace.

A further intimation of the problem can be seen in the way Calvin treats the subject in the *Institutes*. In the final edition, having devoted a chapter to election followed by a second chapter entitled "Confirmation of this Doctrine from Scriptural Testimonies" (*Inst.*, 3, 22), Calvin deemed it necessary to write a third chapter (3, 23)—something that happens no-

---

20. Herder, quoted by Bavinck in *The Doctrine of God*, trans. and ed. William Hendriksen (Grand Rapids: William B. Eerdmans, 1951), p. 356.

21. See *CD*, 2/2: 1–506. Otto Weber allots an independent section to the treatment of election in his dogmatics ("Gottes Gnadenwahle," in *Grundlagen der Dogmatik* [Düsseldorf: Neukirchener Verlag, 1977], 2: 458–566), thus giving the doctrine the same status in his outline as Christology, Pneumatology, and ecclesiology. In fact, the 108 pages he devotes to the subject exceed those he gives to the entire range of eschatology (forty-one pages).

where else in the *Institutes* — entitled "Refutation of the False Accusations with Which This Doctrine Has Always Been Unjustly Burdened." The opening sentence of this third chapter is hardly more reassuring than its title: "Now when human understanding hears these things [concerning election and reprobation], its insolence is so irrepressible that it breaks forth into random and immoderate tumult as if at the blast of a battle trumpet." Zwingli's successor in Zurich, Heinrich Bullinger, wrote privately to Calvin, "Believe me, many are displeased with what you say in your *Institutes* on predestination."[22] (With the passing of time, however, Bullinger moved ever closer to Calvin's doctrine.)

As we noted above, Beza, Calvin's successor in the theological chair at Geneva, found it necessary to spend more time defending Calvin's doctrine of predestination than anything else the master taught. And Beza's best known student, Jacobus Arminius, for all the arguments of the master, was hardly convinced. Later, as a professor of theology in his own right, he delivered several broadsides against the doctrine of predestination echoing the earlier complaints that Phigius, Bolsec, and others had lodged while Calvin was still alive. According to Arminius, a doctrine of predestination that grounds the distinction between the elect and the reprobate in the will of God rather than in the will of the creature (who chooses to believe or disbelieve) is "repugnant to the nature of God" (who is merciful and just), "contrary to the nature of man" (who has freedom of the will), "diametrically opposed to the act of creation," "at open hostility with the nature of eternal life," "opposed to the nature of eternal death," "inconsistent with the nature and properties of sin," "repugnant to the nature of divine grace," "injurious to the glory of God" (since it makes God the real sinner!), "dishonorable to Jesus Christ our Savior," and so on.[23]

The controversy, to be sure, has had its lighter moments. Christopher Ness became a sort of Lewis Carroll in adding new words to the English language:

> The Arminians may be called sub-mortuarians, for their holding no full election till men die; and post-destinarians, for placing the eternal election behind the course of man's life. . . . And may they not also be styled re-lapsarians, for saying that the elect may totally and finally fall away?

And he likewise complains that

> as the emperors wrapped the early Christians in skins and then exposed them to be torn to pieces by their fierce ban-dogs, so do the Arminians with the great truth of predestination. They first dress it

---

22. Bullinger, quoted by Schaff in *History of the Christian Church*, 8 vols. (New York: Scribners, 1910), 8/2: 618.
23. See Arminius, *Writings*, 3 vols., trans. James Nichols (Grand Rapids: Baker, 1956), 1: 221ff.

up in an ugly shape, with their own false glosses upon it, then they let fly at it one cynical sarcasm after another.[24]

And Spurgeon, over 150 years later, charged that "Arminianism marries Christ to a bride he did not choose." But for the most part, the controversy over election has been more than tilting at windmills; it has divided lifelong friends and even whole Christian communions.

Turning from the question of controversy to that of theological methodology, we readily acknowledge that methodology cannot be equated with order *simpliciter*; nevertheless, the two are related, and one can anticipate the approach of a given systematician to the doctrine of election by noting where he locates the materials in his larger treatment. As early as the Gottschalk debate in the ninth century, the term "predestination" began to be used broadly of that which is "predetermined, decreed, preestablished, foreordained" by God.[25] Such a view implies that things as well as persons—indeed, not merely events in salvation history but all of history itself—are predestined, and so election is simply a specific instance of predestination. For those who understood predestination in this general sense as the decree of God, the doctrine of the decree became a part of the doctrine of God, the fundamental doctrine in all theology. Zwingli, for example, held that the entire doctrine of providence was subsumed under the concept of the decree of God. Calvin also tended to treat predestination not only in terms of election to salvation but also in terms of providence.

Calvin's inclination is more pronounced in his successor Beza, who argued that Paul moved by a logical necessity from sanctification to justification to predestination as the ultimate doctrine without which the others could not be understood. While Beza may have been forced to place a major emphasis on predestination because of the polemics of the age, there can be little doubt that many who succeeded him were, in principle, "decretal" theologians.[26] Given such an approach—in which salvation (election) is an instance of providence and providence is the continuation of creation and cre-

---

24. Ness, *An Antidote against Arminianism* (London, 1700), pp. 48, 8.
25. See Jaroslav Pelikan, *The Christian Tradition: A History of the Development of Doctrine*, 3 vols. (Chicago: University of Chicago Press, 1971–78), 3: 85.
26. On the interpretation of Beza in these matters, see J. S. Bray, *Theodore Beza's Doctrine of Predestination* (Nieuwkoop: DeGraaf, 1975), pp. 70–85.

ation is the execution of the divine decree—there is always the danger that God's choice of the sinner will become so basic that the human response to the gospel (i.e., the sinner's choice of God) will lose its significance as a responsible act.

The decretal approach is given confessional status in the Irish Articles (1615) and in the Westminster Confession of Faith (1647). In the latter, the chapter entitled "Of God's Eternal Decree" follows immediately after a chapter on the Trinity and precedes not only the chapter dealing with sin and salvation but even those dealing with creation and providence. In Heppe's *Reformed Dogmatics*, chapter 7, entitled "The Decrees of God," likewise immediately follows a chapter on the Trinity and is followed, in turn, by chapters on predestination, creation, and providence. Heppe has no chapter at all on election as such, the subject having been swallowed up, as it were, in the decrees.[27] Heppe's chapter on the decrees concludes with a reproduction of Beza's celebrated chart: "The Sum of All Christianity; or, The Description and Distribution of the Causes of the Salvation of the Elect and of the Destruction of the Reprobate, Collected from the Sacred Writings." (Barth, who expresses warm appreciation for Heppe's work in his foreword to the 1935 edition, contends that Beza's chart was meant simply to indicate the connection of predestination to other doctrines rather than to show that all other doctrines can be deduced by a logical necessity from predestination [see *CD*, 2/2: 78].)

A more recent example of this sort of approach can be found in the third volume of the Contemporary Evangelical Thought series, entitled *Basic Christian Doctrines*, which places chapters entitled "The Decrees of God" and "Predestination" before the chapter on the Trinity and contains no chapter on election at all.[28]

If one approaches the doctrine of election from the perspective of eternity (*sub specie aeternitatis*), one must keep in mind that the *a priori* methodology to which such an approach easily leads runs the risk of turning the doctrine of predestination into theological axiom and reducing the significance of human history to mere appearance. However, one should not suppose that the opposite methodology, the so-called *a posteriori* approach, which treats election from the perspective of time (*sub specie temporis*), is the antidote to all theological ills. This approach may have the pastoral value of grounding the assurance of one's own election in the historical ex-

---

27. See Heppe, *Reformed Dogmatics*, trans. G. T. Thomson (1861; London: Allen & Unwin, 1950).

28. *Basic Christian Doctrines*, ed. C. F. Henry (New York: Holt, Rinehart & Winston, 1962)

perience of one's calling, but when pressed to extremes, it gives meaning and significance to human history only at the expense of the divine agency and purpose. The emphasis it places on the human agent's choosing the Savior becomes so basic that the emphasis on God's choosing the sinner is reduced, for all practical purposes, to mere appearance. In other words, it conceives of the divine purpose as not a *purpose* at all but mere prescience, divine foresight of what will happen by human choice. The only purpose left that may be described as God's purpose is his decision to accept the foreseen decision of the creature. This really drains election of all significance, for it is the choice at the human level—belief or unbelief— foreseen, perhaps, but not foreordained, that constitutes the basis of "election." One is not chosen from "before the foundation of the world"; rather, one's choice of Christ is foreseen "from before the foundation of the world."

When it comes to election, one may indeed work inductively from the fruit to the root or deductively from the root to the fruit; but regardless of one's approach to understanding the doctrine, the root in fact precedes the fruit: one is elect before one is called. Hence, whatever obvious pastoral benefits may accrue to one's working from the point of salvation experienced to the point of salvation planned, systematicians cannot confine themselves to this method and still work competently; that is why the great theologians have worked the other way. To put matters in everyday language, they have assumed that salvation is God's work, not the creature's. In the words of the psalmist, salvation ("deliverance," "rescue," "well-being") is of the Lord (Ps. 3:8). Our doctrine of salvation must be grounded in our doctrine of God, which means that our doctrine of election must be grounded in our doctrine of the *will* of God. Election is God's choice, not the sinner's choice.

As we seek to work out the doctrine of election as best we can, then, we will be proceeding on the basis of these assumptions. This is not to say that we would place the doctrine of election immediately after the doctrine of the Trinity in our systematics, but we would surely place it before the doctrine of salvation considered in its historical outworking. In summary, we regard election as much more than merely a divine echo of the choice the sinner makes. At the same time, we will have to acknowledge that the human choice is not a choice in name only; clearly it does have meaning for time and eternity. A middle course between the two extremes weighted on the divine side would seem to have the most promise of providing the Thesean thread that will lead us out of the maze of theological difficulty.

Speaking of method and location, it is interesting to note where the Methodist Richard Watson locates the doctrine of election in his *Theological Institutes* (1823). Written, as the name implies, in conscious refutation of Calvin's *Institutes* (there are two volumes totaling 1,330 pages), it contains a "Table of Contents" that does not so much as mention the divine decree, predestination, creation, providence, or election. In a document entitled "Detailed Analysis" published with the thirtieth edition in 1879, one can finally track down the treatment of election. It is taken up in a section entitled "The Extent of Redemption," a sub-subsection under the heading of "Doctrines Relating to Man." Here we read, "What is the import of that act of grace which is termed 'an election?' " And the answer is given, "To be elected is to be separated from the world," and to be "sanctified by the Spirit and by the blood of Christ; hence election is not only an *act done in time*, but subsequent to the administration of the means of salvation." Election, in other words, is not an eternal decision but a temporal act. And it comes not "before the foundation of the world" but "subsequent to the administration of the means of salvation"—that is, after the preaching of the word. And Watson, it should be noted, is not talking about the sinner's *awareness* of his or her election, but of election itself. Such an approach treats the subject *sub specie temporis* with a consistency that deserves the name "*post*destinarianism."

1. Election and Foreknowledge

As we turn to the various statements of the doctrine of election and the individual, statements over which the theologians have labored and disputed through the years, we shall attempt first to summarize them as clearly as possible and then to offer comments on their relative merits in the light of Scripture. This is no easy task, for the question of individual election has led more people to read Scripture for what they want to find (rather than to listen to Scripture for what they are afraid to hear) than virtually any other theological issue. Just to review the nuances of the argument threatens to make one a mere dilettante in the realm of possibilities. But where nothing is ventured, nothing is gained, and so we shall proceed with our task. Our ordering and interpretation of the data will reflect the methodological distinction to which we have frequently alluded—approaching the subject *sub specie temporis* as against approaching it *sub specie aeternitatis*. The former method, sometimes called the historical or *a posteriori* approach, undoubtedly has the oldest pedigree, and so we shall begin with it.[29]

This is the approach that the ancient Greek Fathers favored. They sought, for the most part, to resolve the problem of election and the reprobation it implies by inferring that since God wills the salvation of all, offers it to all, and holds those to be without excuse who reject it, his predestination must be based on his foreknowledge of who will and who will not accept the grace offered in Christ.[30]

> Prescience effectively removed the objections to the doctrine of predestination, although embedding the definition of the elect in a doctrine of prescience removed the doctrine of predestination itself from any central position. The term "God's changeless will from eternity" now referred not to the eternal predestinating will by which God had chosen some and rejected others, but to the will spoken of in 1 Timothy 2:4, that all men be saved. This, and not predestination, was now to be called an "essential element of the faith [pars fidei]" and "a rule of apostolic doctrine."[31]

This position that embraces election in the doctrine of the divine prescience has remained virtually unchanged down to the present in Greek Orthodoxy. It is summed up in the authoritative pronouncement of the Orthodox Catechism of the Eastern Church as follows:

> Q. 121: Has not that will of God, by which man is designed for eternal happiness, its own proper name in theology?

---

29. The position of which we speak, which views election from the perspective of time, should not be confused with the argument that the double issue at the end of time—sheep and goats, acquittal and condemnation, heaven and hell—implies a double decree from eternity. Augustine draws such an inference, as does Calvin, but Barth rejects it. We should note, however, that in his zeal to correct the Augustinian doctrine at this point, Barth so emphasizes a universalism from the beginning of history (suggesting that all are elect from eternity by and in Christ) that he has difficulty in escaping universalism *(apokatastasis)* at the end of history (see *CD*, 2/2: 37ff.; Brunner, Dogmatics, 1: 349ff.).

30. This coordination of the human will with divine grace was consonant with their emphasis on free will as the power of contrary choice *(liberium arbitrium indifferentiae)* over against pagan Greek fatalism. Since it was grace that the elect accepted they could not boast their own merit before God, and since it was the free choice of the reprobate to reject this grace, they could not accuse the divine justice in condemning them.

31. Pelikan, *The Christian Tradition*, 1: 326–27.

A. It is called the predestination of God. . . .

Q. 125: How does the Orthodox church speak on this point?

A. In the exposition of the faith of the Eastern Patriarchs it is said: As he foresaw that some would use well their free will, but others ill, he accordingly predestined the former to glory, while the latter he condemned.[32]

This Eastern Orthodox position, which was framed in conscious rejection of Augustinianism, is parallel in many ways to that of the early Arminians of Holland, who framed their doctrine in conscious rejection of Dutch Calvinism. Like the Eastern church, Arminius repeatedly grounds predestination (a term he approves and freely uses) in the divine foreknowledge. God never "absolutely" predestines anyone to salvation, says Arminius, but rather "conditionally" predestines them, in the sense that he contemplates them as believers. Arminius accuses the Calvinistic doctrine of violating the basic freedom of the will endemic to our humanity as created by God. He maintains that

> the first absolute decree is the appointment of Jesus Christ as Redeemer; the second, to receive all who believe in him and condemn all who disbelieve; and the third, to administer to all, in a sufficient and efficacious manner, the means to salvation.
>
> To these succeeds the fourth decree, by which God decreed to save and damn certain particular persons. This decree has its foundations in the foreknowledge of God by which he knew from all eternity those individuals who would, through his preventing grace, *believe*, and, through his subsequent grace *would persevere* . . ., and, by which foreknowledge, he likewise knew those who *would not believe and persevere*.[33]

Among Protestants, the position that bases God's election and rejection on his foreknowledge has long had an appeal, particularly among those who are in the Arminian and Wesleyan traditions. Indeed, among lay students of Scripture it is probably the most widely held view. One might ask, then, why more theologians have not accepted

---

32. The Larger Catechism of the Orthodox, Catholic, Eastern Church, cited in Schaff, *The Greek and Latin Creeds*, vol. 2 of *Bibliotheca symbolica ecclesiae universalis*, pp. 464–65.

33. Arminius, "My Own Sentiments on Predestination," in Writings, 1: 247–48; italics his. See also 1: 221ff.

it; and some might even wonder if such disparity between a lay and a professional understanding of Scripture does not indict the latter as an irrelevant luxury.

In response, it should be acknowledged that the *sub specie temporis* approach does have about it a *prima facie* plausibility. It can easily be inferred from a fundamental strand of biblical revelation: the Scriptures plainly teach that a genuine offer of salvation is made to all in the gospel (Matt. 28:19–20), that the gospel itself is the good news that Christ died for all (2 Cor. 5:14–15), and that this death commends the love of a God (Rom. 5:8) who wills the salvation of all (1 Tim. 2:4). If God is the seeking God, the God who all day long stretches forth his hands to rebellious sinners (Isa. 65:2; Rom. 10:21), the God who solemnly declares that he has no pleasure in the death of the wicked (Ezek. 33:11), what other position can one take? The fact that some are and others are not the beneficiaries of his grace must, in the last analysis, be attributed to the free decision of the creature either to accept or to reject the grace freely offered in the gospel. At least so it would seem.

At this juncture some may wonder that the passages often cited as proof texts for an election based on foreknowledge have not been included in this discussion: "Whom he did *foreknow*, he also did predestinate" (Rom. 8:29, KJV); Christians are "elect according to the *foreknowledge* of God the Father" (1 Pet. 1:2, KJV). The answer is simply that these texts do not say "Whom God foreknew *would believe*, he predestinated," nor that we as Christians are "elect according to the foreknowledge *which God has of our faith*."

Not only are such additions to the text gratuitous, but even the lexicographers (not to mention the dogmaticians) recognize that the Greek words occurring in these texts (προγινοσκω, προγνωσις) refer to God's "fixing his attention upon beforehand"; they are terms that have to do with God's omniscient wisdom and purpose. Hence, in his *Greek-English Lexicon of the New Testament*, Bauer translates Romans 8:29 "Whom he chose beforehand" and 1 Peter 1:2 "Elect according to the predestination of God the Father." (See also the RSV rendering of 1 Pet. 1:2: "chosen and destined by God the Father.")

Plausible as the ancient view of an election based on the divine prescience may be, however, it is not without significant problems. Not the least of these problems is that it provides no convincing interpretation of that strand of revelation to which Augustine and his followers appealed. As we have observed, the Greek Fathers largely ignored Augustine's doctrine of predestination. To do this they also had to ignore in large part the Scripture on which his doctrine is based. And those extensive and quite clear portions of Scripture that they could not ignore, they palpably misinterpreted.

Origen, for example, attributes Romans 9:14–19 (in which Paul says that God "has mercy on whomever he will and hardens whomever he will") to an opponent whom the apostle is refuting! God calls people because they are worthy, he says; therefore, it cannot be said that they are worthy because they are called. And he goes on to contend that they are worthy to be called because they have made themselves so in a state of preexistence. Chrysostom, whose interpretation of Romans 9 is similar to that of Origen (sans reincarnation), says that Jacob was called because he was worthy and known to be such in the divine foreknowledge. He explains the phrase, "the purpose of God according to election" (v. 11), as meaning, "the election which is according to God's purpose and foreknowledge," a remarkable display of exegetical legerdemain.[34]

As one ponders this early Eastern interpretation of Romans 9, one cannot help but observe that such a meaning would have given Paul a ready answer to the question he puts on the lips of his reader: "You will say to me then, 'Why does he [God] still find fault? For who can resist his will?' " (v. 19). Had he in fact been thinking along the lines of Origen and Chrysostom, he would not have reminded us that we should not answer back to God, whose power is like that of a potter over his clay (9:20ff.) but should instead have said, "Such a question reflects a fundamental misunderstanding of my argument. I quite agree that all are free to resist his will. Ergo, God has

---

34. William Sanday and Arthur C. Headlam observe that Origen's commentary greatly influenced Chrysostom and that Chrysostom's commentaries became supreme in the East and largely influenced all later Greek and Russian commentators down to the present time (A *Critical and Exegetical Commentary on the Epistle to the Romans*, International Critical Commentary [New York: Scribners, 1896], pp. 269ff.). No modern Protestant scholars, we might observe, would thus manipulate the text. But some have found it equally difficult to accept. William Barclay, for example, comments on Paul's argument in Romans 9 that not only is it "invalid," but it "is one at which the mind staggers and from which we quite properly recoil" (*The Letter to the Romans*, Daily Study Bible [Philadelphia: Westminster, 1975], p. 120).

every reason to find fault with those whom he foresees will use their freedom to resist him."

Arminius's handling of the text of Romans 9 is only a little less arbitrary than that of the Eastern Fathers. Ishmael and Esau are types of those who seek salvation by works, he argues, as Isaac and Jacob are types of those who seek it by faith. While it is true that only those who seek salvation by faith will be saved, we cannot infer that Ishmael and Esau are not saved, for what pertains to the antitype does not necessarily pertain to the type. Furthermore, he argues, it clearly cannot be maintained that Romans 9 is speaking of an eternal decree by which some are elected to salvation and others are rejected solely on the basis of the divine will. To the contrary, the purpose of this chapter, and indeed of the whole epistle, is to set forth the doctrine of salvation by faith in contrast to the doctrine of salvation by works. Hence, he concludes that the only purpose or decree of God being referred to here is his immutable determination, made from all eternity, to save those whom he foresees will have faith in Christ, and those alone.

This argument of Arminius that election is based on foreseen faith is so poorly graduated to the thought of Romans 9 that it can hardly convince one who does not have the will to believe. When Paul argues, for example, that answering back to God is like the clay talking back to the potter, who obviously has the right "to make out of the same lump one vessel to honor and another to dishonor" (vv. 20–21), Arminius sees a reference to creation rather than to salvation: God made the man and the woman to be vessels of honor, but they made themselves vessels of dishonor "without any concurrence of the Deity," he says. He goes on to argue that the divine wisdom and goodness found a way to remedy the situation in Jesus Christ, and thus that those who persist in evil are of necessity made—or, rather, make themselves—vessels of wrath. "God makes man a vessel, man makes himself an evil vessel or a sinner."[35]

But such details of exegesis only point up the more fundamental and obvious problem with the argument that election is based on divine foreknowledge—namely, that such a position is in fact simply a way of saying that God does not really elect or reject anyone

---

35. See his "Analysis of the Ninth Chapter of the Epistle to the Romans," *Writings*, 3: 527ff. The discussion of the potter and the clay is found on pp. 554ff.

but that from eternity he simply resolves to actualize a general redemptive purpose that incidentally gives rise to a distinction among men and women. Naturally God knows from all eternity that such a distinction will occur; and by his proceeding to embrace such a distinction in his purpose, he affirms it. Thus, says Arminius, we may in this sense say that there is an election and rejection according to God's purpose, but to do so is not to suggest that the initiative in the selection is his. Rather, the initiative is with the creature. Instead of a free *divine* election *in* Christ, there is a free *human* election *of* Christ.

This is the subtle *quid pro quo* of the argument that makes it, for all its ancient pedigree and popular appeal, unacceptable to those who are in the Augustinian and Reformed tradition.[36] The Scriptures say that God chose us in Christ from before the foundation of the world (Eph. 1:4), not that he saw us from before the foundation of the world as choosing Christ. There is no possible way of reducing these two statements to a common meaning. They are not even similar in meaning. As might be expected, therefore, there is another view of the doctrine of election, a view quite different from what we have been considering to this point. This other view holds that election is a matter not of divine foresight but rather of divine foreordination, that its ultimate ground is the free choice of God, not the foreseen choice of the sinner. We shall presently give our attention to this view, but first a brief word on election and the freedom of the will is in order.

Addendum: Election and Free Will

As creatures made in the image of God, human beings are not merely free to determine this or that about themselves but are free to determine themselves as selves. Yet this freedom of self-determination is not ultimate in the Christian view, for it is God who has made us and not we ourselves (Ps. 100:3). Since we are who we are,

---

36. This subtle transfer of the emphasis from the eternal, divine decision to the temporal, human decision is found not only in the Arminian and Wesleyan traditions but in the Lutheran and Anglo-Catholic traditions as well, which contend that God in his electing grace contemplates (foresees) those who will "believe and be baptized," those who will "improve the grace of their baptism," and so forth.

as human, by the act of our Creator, we acknowledge that our freedom is a divine gift and that we are accountable to God for the use we make of it. The discussion of these and related matters belongs properly to the locus of anthropology. Yet obviously the questions of election and free will impinge upon each other, as is evidenced by the fact that from the time of Augustine, many have felt that his doctrine of election violates the creature's freedom of self-determination.

At this juncture we should recall the nature of original sin as Augustine came to understand it. Although humankind was created with original righteousness and therefore able not to sin (*posse non peccare*), as a result of the fall all are born sinners, according to Augustine, and therefore not able not to sin (*non posse non peccare*). Hence no one, apart from grace, is free to be other than a sinner.

Augustine, then, unlike the Greek Fathers, holds that freedom resides not in the power of contrary choice (*liberium arbitrium indifferentiae*), but in the power of self-determination within the limits of one's sinful human nature: it is freedom not from our (sinful) selves but from coercion by outside powers alien to ourselves. The divine power is, indeed, other than our own, but it is not alien to it. In this respect, as in all others, the relationship of the creature to the Creator is *sui generis*. At the human level, to be sure, the "I" and the "thou" are autonomous vis-à-vis each other. Hence, we mutually experience the will of the "other" as outside our own and alien to it. For this reason, we can impose our will on another only by some form of coercion that violates the freedom of the other. But at the divine/human level this situation does not prevail. Since there is no *possibility* that the creature could impose his or her will on the Creator ("Why do the nations conspire and the peoples plot in vain?" Ps. 2:1), so there is no need that the Creator should impose his will on the creature. And why? Because it is in him that we "live and move and have our being" (Acts 17:28) as human beings. God, then, "works in us," not outside us, much less against us, "to will and to work for his good pleasure" (Phil. 2:13).

As a result of this view of the matter, Augustine, and those who follow him in his teaching on predestination, have never struggled with the Scriptures that say (or imply) that "whosoever will may come."[37] No one argues that those who wish to come to Christ may be refused. The question is how sinners can be willing to come in the first place, and the answer is that God has made them willing in the day of his power, giving them a new heart and thereby renewing their wills. Hence Charles Wesley (Arminian though he was) has rightly taught us to sing,

> He wills that I should holy be:
> Who can withstand his will;
> The counsels of this grace in me
> He surely shall fulfill!

Consequently, when it comes to predestination and free will, the Eastern Orthodox and Arminians on the one side, and the Augustinians and Calvinists on the other, have often been like ships passing in the night. Their differing views of human freedom make what appears to one side a surmountable problem seem to the other side quite insurmountable. (The real difficulty for the Augustinian predestinarian, as we shall see, is not the relating of the divine will to the human, but the relating of the divine will to the divine love in the case of the reprobate.) Nevertheless, the protest that Augustine's doctrine of predestination violates human free will does not altogether miss the mark, especially when the implications of double predestination are pressed to logical extremes, as in certain forms of decretal theology.[38]

We shall have more to say about these matters later; at this point it will be enough simply to observe that the doctrine of creation implies that the human will is grounded in the divine will. Had God not willed that we should be and that we should be free, we would

---

37. While this oft-quoted phrase from the popular hymn of P. P. Bliss is not the *ipsissima verba* of Scripture, it is surely the implication of Scripture (see especially Rev. 22:17, in which the KJV translates ο θελων λαβετω υδωρ ζωης δωρεαν, "and whosoever will, let him take the water of life freely."

38. In 1903, American Presbyterians added a "Declaratory Statement" to the Westminster Confession with reference to chapter 3, "Of God's Eternal Decree." It reads in part, "the Presbyterian Church . . . does authoritatively declare as follows: that men are fully responsible for their treatment of God's gracious offer; that his decree hinders no man from accepting that offer; and that no man is condemned except on the ground of his sin." While such a pronouncement is not intended to solve every problem, it is at least a tacit admission that one exists.

not exist as free agents. Our freedom, then, is not that of independence, but of dependence on him who made and sustains us and all his creatures. In addition, since he has made us as *persons*, we can assume that his will for us is not realized in the form of "destiny"—that is, he does not determine our wills in the same way that he determines the color of our skin or the pattern of our hair. He does not compel the Yes of his elect to the offer of his grace; rather, he *wins* it. In the case of the reprobate, he does not compel their No to the same offer; rather, he *confirms* it.

How this can be we cannot say. We understand by experience what we cannot fathom by rational analysis.[39] We know experientially what the Scriptures mean when they speak of the choice Joshua and his house made to serve the Lord rather than the gods of Mesopotamia and Canaan (Josh. 24:15). Similarly, we know the meaning of the command to choose to serve Christ as Lord rather than the gods of this world with which the gospel confronts us. Yet we do not stand before that choice as one of several possibilities, as though we were selecting items from a menu in a restaurant. In other words, we do not become aware that we are elect as we become aware that we are fair-haired or dark-haired; rather, our awareness involves a real and momentous choice on our part. We not only recognize that we have been chosen; we choose our having been chosen. We elect, as it were, our having been elected. To the question "Will you also go away?" the answer is "Lord, to whom shall we go?" (John 6:67–68). To confess Jesus' name is to know both the freedom that name gives to us and also the power it wields in us.

> He moved my soul to seek him, seeking me;
> It was not I that found, O Savior true;
> No, I was found of thee. . . .
> For thou wert long beforehand with my soul;
> Always thou lovedst me.
>
> —*Anon.*

---

39. Commenting on Paul's argument in Romans 9–11, Barclay observes, "He sets two things side by side; everything is of God and everything is of human choice. Paul makes no attempt to resolve this dilemma; and the fact is that there is no resolution of it. . . . We know that God is behind everything; and yet, at the same time, we know that we have free will and can accept or reject God's offer. It is the paradox of the human situation that God is in control and yet the human will is free" *(The Letter to the Romans*, p. 143).

2. Election and Predestination

In the approach to election that has prevailed in the Eastern tradition (and in parts of the Western tradition as well), the distinction between the elect and the reprobate is grounded in the choice of the creature: God elects and rejects on the basis of his all-encompassing foreknowledge of the creature's choice. Given such a view, in which the human choice determines the divine, time reaches back into eternity, and eternity, so to speak, becomes "laden with time." Arminius, who has given his name to this approach in Protestant circles, declared that "predestination, when thus explained, is the foundation of Christianity . . . the sum and the matter of the gospel; nay it is the gospel itself."[40] But is his claim to have "explained" predestination by basing it on foreknowledge justified? I would suggest that it is. We may or may not agree that his doctrine is biblical, that his exegesis is sound, but we can hardly doubt that it makes sense in its own right, that it resolves the problem. It is a consistent inference from his fundamental premise, the premise on which the Greek Fathers approached the question from the beginning—namely, that human freedom consists in the power of contrary choice. According to Arminius, to be human is to be free to determine one's own destiny in the ultimate sense of the word, and hence, though he may have explained it *away*, he has, in fact, explained predestination.

Standing over against this view is the view that the divine choice determines the human choice, that eternity, as it were, breaks into time, that time becomes "laden with eternity." To focus the either/or with which this view confronts us as clearly as possible, we shall consider this second position in its most consistent and logically compelling form—that is, in the form of double predestination, the doctrine that God has predestinated some to salvation and others to condemnation. Given such a position, God's will is clearly the final reason that some are elect and some reprobate. The freedom of the creature is grounded in the freedom of the Creator, whose prerogative it is to determine the destiny of the creature according to his infinite wisdom. In my judgment, this Augustinian approach reflects a much more impressive biblical and exegetical effort than does the Pelagian and Arminian view. Furthermore, the proponents of this view, though

---

40. Arminius, *Writings*, 1: 248.

gifted with profound theological minds, have for the most part been humble enough to use the word "mystery" rather than "explanation" when describing their formulations of the doctrine. Yet running through the discussion in their case also is a sustained effort to "explain," to "understand," to draw out the logical implications of the fundamental premise with which Augustine began—namely, the sovereignty of God.

Setting forth this view is a demanding exercise, for the many ways in which it has been formulated entail a host of different nuances, the evidence of a thrust toward logical consistency being less in some and more in others. While this tendency toward rational explanation varies, depending on who is arguing with whom, we can simplify the situation without undue distortion by looking at the matter chronologically.

The doctrine of double predestination is clearly articulated in the works of Augustine; it is reaffirmed subsequently by Gottschalk and others in the Western church who, as a minority, urged his position against the semi-Augustinian majority in the Middle Ages; and finally it is espoused by the Protestant Reformers and those who followed them. In essence the doctrine states that God predestines some to life (the elect) and some to death (the reprobate) with the notable difference that the elect are predestined to life though they do *not* deserve it, while the reprobate are condemned to death because they *do* deserve it. This characterization underscores the asymmetry at that heart of the doctrine with which the predestinarians have struggled the most; their efforts to overcome this asymmetry is what I had in mind when I suggested that running through the discussion is a tendency to "explain" the doctrine by pressing the logical implications of the divine sovereignty.

This tendency toward explanation is most sharply focused, not by the doctrine of election as such, but by its counterpart, the doctrine of reprobation. As we noted in our survey of the biblical data, divine election implies rejection. But how are we to speak of this divine rejection? To ask this question is to put one's finger on the Achilles' heel of the argument for double predestination. The first intimation of difficulty can be found in Augustine's insistence that while God predestines the sinner to perdition, he does not predestine the creature to sin. But it was not until the Protestant Reformers returned to the Augustinian doctrine of grace that the stage was set for an in-depth discussion of the problem implied in this distinction. We shall, therefore, begin our analysis with the Reformers—and with Calvin rather than Luther, since the latter's doctrine of the *Deus absconditus* would involve not only the question of election and reprobation but also his attempt to synthesize divine love and wrath, a subject too large for our present purpose. In any case, Calvin has been the primary mentor in the Reformed tradition, in which the doctrine of "the rejected" has received the most attention.

Calvin's Doctrine Summarized

Like Luther, Calvin was firmly committed to the Augustinian interpretation of Paul's doctrine of grace. He was a double predestinarian, asserting that as the salvation of the elect is God's work, so is the condemnation of the reprobate. But is there no difference between them? Did the God of Calvin create the reprobate "in order to hurry them from the womb to the tomb, to everlasting doom" as Schaff suggests? As an honest and competent exegete, Calvin halts between two opinions in his *Commentaries*. When he comes to the difficult text on the election of Jacob and rejection of Esau (Rom. 9:10–13), he comments,

> When, therefore, Paul says that neither of them had at that time done any good or evil, we must add at the same time his assumption that they were both the children of Adam, sinners by nature, and not possessed of a particle of righteousness.[41]

In other words, though Esau (and all of whom he is the type) are not rejected for their personal sins, nonetheless they are rejected as sinners in Adam. "The Lord, in His unmerited election," Calvin reminds us, "is free and exempt from the necessity of bestowing equally the same grace on all. Rather, He passes by those whom He wills, and chooses whom he wills."[42]

Calvin argues in the same way in the *Institutes*:

---

41. Calvin, *The Epistles of Paul the Apostle to the Romans and the Thessalonians*, trans. Ross Mackenzie, Calvin's New Testament Commentaries, ed. David W. Torrance and Thomas F. Torrance (Edinburgh: Oliver & Boyd, 1960), p. 200.

42. Calvin, *The Epistles of Paul the Apostle to the Romans and the Thessalonians*, p. 200.

> As all of us are vitiated by sin, we can only be odious to God, and that not from tyrannical cruelty but by the fairest reckoning of justice. But if all whom the Lord predestines to death are by condition of nature subject to the judgment of death, of what injustice toward themselves may they complain?
> . . . If all are drawn from a corrupt mass, no wonder they are subject to condemnation! (*Inst.*, 3, 23, 3)

Calvin's reference to the reprobate as "passed by" and left to a just condemnation as part of the "corrupt mass" (*massa corrupta*) of fallen humanity reflects a way of speaking that became a standard part of Reformed doctrine. It is suggested by Paul's reference to the potter and the clay in Romans 9:21ff. As the potter shapes one vessel to honor and another to dishonor, working with the same lump of clay (εκ του αυτου φυραματος), so God, of the same lump (mass) of sinful humanity, shapes vessels of wrath (the reprobate) and of mercy (the elect).

> Behold the potter and the clay!
> He forms his vessels as he please;
> Such is our God and such are we,
> The subjects of his just decrees.
> —*Watts*

Modern commentators have objected that the analogy the apostle uses is a bad one. C. H. Dodd, for example, states that "It [Rom. 9:21] is the weakest part in the whole epistle."[43] But if the sovereignty of God in creation and redemption is taken seriously, then the analogy is quite in order. No one especially objects to Jeremiah's use of the image in saying that the potter breaks the defective vessel in order to make it new (Jer. 18:4–5). Obviously it is the doctrine that the apostle seems to teach rather than the analogy he uses in teaching it that evokes such a response on the part of many moderns. Human beings are responsible agents, not lumps of clay, as Barclay and others remind us.

But there is another strand of reasoning in Calvin that does not contradict and yet surely goes beyond the thought that the reprobate are sinners belonging to the corrupt mass of fallen humanity and therefore left to a just condemnation. Still speaking of Jacob and Esau (Rom. 9:11), Calvin goes on to say that while it is indeed true that

> the immediate cause of reprobation is the curse which we all inherit from Adam. Nevertheless, Paul withdraws us from this view, so that

---

43. Dodd, *The Epistle to the Romans*, Moffatt Commentary (London: Hodder & Stoughton, 1932), p. 59.

ELECTION AND THE INDIVIDUAL

> we may learn to acquiesce in the bare and simple good pleasure of God, until he has established the doctrine that God has a sufficiently just reason for election and reprobation in His own will.[44]

And so, by shifting the argument from the divine justice to the divine will, Calvin overcomes the asymmetry in the doctrine of double predestination we noted previously. As the elect are predestined to life apart from any consideration of their merit, so the reprobate are predestined to death apart from any consideration of their *de*merit. In both instances it is ultimately a matter of the divine will as sovereign.

Nor is this an incidental comment on a specific text. Rather, it is a major part of Calvin's doctrine. In the *Institutes* he plainly teaches that since all the descendants of Adam fell by the divine will, when we raise the question of the condemnation of the reprobate, "we must always at last return to the sole decision of God's will, the cause of which is hidden in him" (*Inst.*, 3, 23, 4). It is true that Romans 9:22ff. speaks simply of there being vessels of wrath as "made for destruction," but includes no specific remarks concerning their origin, whereas the vessels of mercy for glory are specifically said to have been prepared by God. But Calvin dismisses this difference, maintaining that although by "using a different expression [Paul] softens the harshness of the former clause, it is utterly inconsistent to transfer the preparation for destruction to anything but God's secret plan" (*Inst.*, 3, 23, 1). He goes on to say,

> What of those, then, whom he created for dishonor in life and destruction in death, to become the instruments of his wrath and examples of his severity? That they may come to their end, he sometimes deprives them of the capacity to hear his word; at other times he, rather, blinds and stuns them by the preaching of it. (*Inst.*, 3, 24, 12)[45]

---

44. Calvin, *The Epistles of Paul the Apostle to the Romans and the Thessalonians*, pp. 200–201. At this point in an earlier edition of the commentary, the editor and translator, the Rev. John Owen, vicar of Thussington, Leicestershire, lodges a typical demur: he complains, Calvin and many other divines seem to have gone "somewhat beyond the limits of revelation; it is true, by a process of reasoning apparently obvious; but when we begin to reason on this high and mysterious subject, we become soon bewildered and lost in mazes of difficulty."

45. Calvin proceeds to allude to such passages as Isaiah 6:9–10, in which it is stated that prophets were sent to a people with a message that they were told beforehand the people would not hear; Exodus 4:19, in which Moses is told to

ELECTION AND PREDESTINATION

It would be presumptuous for us even to inquire into the cause of the divine will in this matter, says Calvin,

> For his will is, and rightly ought to be, the cause of all things that are. . . . For God's will is so much the highest rule of righteousness that whatever he wills, by the very fact that he wills it, must be considered righteous. (*Inst.*, 3, 23, 2)[46]

This reasoning leads Calvin, reluctantly but candidly, to confess that the doctrine of reprobation is a *decretum horribile*:

> The decree is dreadful, I confess. Yet no one can deny that God foreknew what end man was to have before he created him, and consequently foreknew because he so ordained by his decree. (*Inst.*, 3, 23, 7)[47]

We must remember that Calvin spoke as he did because his conscience was held fast by the Scriptures he had adduced. And the logical consistency he achieved in stating the decree of double predestination is a tribute to the rigor of his thought, even as his confession that it was "horrible" is a tribute to the sensibility of his heart. Yet one cannot but wonder if he forgot his own warning in which he reminds us that

> the predestination of God is truly a labyrinth from which the mind of man is wholly incapable of extricating itself. But the curiosity of

---

declare the Lord's will to Pharaoh even though God would harden his heart so that he would not obey; and Mark 4:10–13, in which Jesus indicates that he uses parables in order that (ἵνα of purpose) "those outside" the kingdom might not understand. Many contemporary exegetes respond to this view of the "mystery of the kingdom" as they do to Paul's argument in Romans 9: they simply reject it as "certainly not going back to the historical Jesus" (see, for example, G. Bornkamm, *Jesus von Nazareth* [Stuttgart: Kohlhammer, 1956], p. 64).

46. Again and again Calvin observes that the reason for God's will is his own secret and that it is folly for the creature to probe the secret recesses of the divine counsel. Yet, he asks (quoting Augustine), "Must that which is manifest be denied because that which is hidden cannot be comprehended?" (*Inst.*, 3, 23, 13). One is reminded of Watts's rhetorical query,

> Shall man reply against the Lord
>   And call his Maker's ways unjust,
> The thunder of whose dreadful word
>   Can crush a thousand worlds to dust?

47. The vehement protest of Castello, "Put forth now your violence against God who hurls innocent babes even from their mothers' breasts into eternal death," was evoked by the fact that Calvin did not believe all infants dying in infancy were elect (see Schaff, *History of the Christian Church*, 8: 568n.3).

man is so insistent that the more dangerous it is to inquire into a subject, the more boldly he rushes to do so.[48]

Here the proverb "Physician, heal yourself" seems apropos.

Fortunately Calvin had other things to say about predestination that do not compel one to use the adjective "horrible." But before we turn to these other things, we must pause to review the debate that his thoughts on the doctrine of reprobation precipitated—namely, the dispute between the supra- and infralapsarians, a dispute that dominated Reformed theology in the seventeenth century and provides the key to understanding much of Barth's thought as a supralapsarian in the present century.

The Supralapsarian/Infralapsarian Debate

As the name implies, the lapsarian debate has to do with the place of the fall in the electing purpose of God (*lapsarian* from the Latin *lapsare* = "fall"; *supralapsarian* = "before the fall"; *infralapsarian* = "after the fall"). Specifically the question is whether God elected some and rejected others apart from any consideration of their merit, simply because it was his sovereign pleasure so to do, or whether he contemplated the human race as fallen and sinful when he made the choice, electing some to life and passing by others whom he left to a just condemnation for their sin. Those who take the former position are supralapsarians; those who take the latter view are infralapsarians. As we have already noted in considering Calvin, the former view is the more inwardly coherent. Given such a view, the difference between the elect and the reprobate is due in the final analysis to God's mysterious purpose to show his mercy in the elect and his severity in the reprobate. Here the *sub specie aeternitatis* approach to the question of election and reprobation is given its most consistent expression. To appreciate its inner consistency fully, however, we need to elaborate the supralapsarian position in the larger context of a discussion of the divine purpose.

All Christians believe, in some sense, that God has a purpose; but in the Augustinian and Calvinistic tradition the doctrine of an infallible divine purpose has had a central place. God is the God

---

48. Calvin, *The Epistles of Paul the Apostle to the Romans and the Thessalonians*, p. 202.

who declares, "I reveal the end from the beginning, from ancient times I reveal what is to be; I say, 'My purpose shall take effect, I will accomplish all that I please' " (Isa. 46:10, NEB). This purpose of God is achieved through his creation and his providential rule over all. Though human history is marred by the tragedy of sin and death, even this sinful history does not frustrate, but rather accomplishes, the ultimate purpose of God. In and through humankind's fallen and sinful history God works to bring about his salvation history. This salvation history looks beyond itself to a new order in which mercy shall triumph in the fellowship of the redeemed and justice prevail in the judgment of the unrepentant. Thus in all that happens, from the creation and the fall to the covenant made with Abraham and his seed, the incarnation of the Son, the effusion of the Spirit at Pentecost, the formation of the Christian church, and the final consummation in the day of resurrection and judgment, God is at work fulfilling the purpose he fixed upon *from the beginning*. And so all that happens redounds to God's glory. It was in this confidence that the apostle Paul first said what countless Christians have said after him: "We know that in everything God works for good with those who love him, who are called according to his purpose" (Rom. 8:28).

The plain implication of such a position is that the fall of humankind is embraced somehow in the larger divine purpose. But how? The supralapsarian answers that God ordained the fall of humankind, even as he ordained their creation, in order to achieve his *ultimate* purpose of election and reprobation. In other words, the purpose of election and reprobation is logically antecedent to (*supra*) the purpose of the fall. The object God contemplates in his predestinating purpose is humankind as creatable and fallible (*homo creabilis et labilis*). The infralapsarian, on the other hand, reverses this sequence, holding election and reprobation to be logically consequent upon (*infra*) the fall so far as the divine purpose is concerned. The object of God's predestination, then, is humankind as created and fallen *(homo creatus et lapsus)*.

We should note at this juncture that we are speaking not of a temporal but of a *logical* order. We are concerned with the question of the divine purpose as such, not the carrying out of that purpose in time. Obviously God could neither save the elect nor condemn the reprobate before their creation and fall into sin, any more than he could raise Jesus from the dead before he was crucified. But, say the supralapsarians, when the infralapsarians make the logical order of God's thought to be the same as the temporal order in which he carries it out, they are obviously inconsistent.[49]

This rational fallacy at the heart of the infralapsarian position, that the logical order of the divine purpose is the same as the temporal order of its fulfillment, leads to the *reductio ad absurdum* that God purposed to create the world without having decided what he would do with it. Even the human creature, who is only the image of God, does not act in this manner: a wise builder will not begin to build what he cannot finish, nor a king engage in a battle he cannot win (Luke 14:28ff.).

On this point Barth accuses infralapsarianism of being not only illogical but unbiblical. To say we cannot know God's original purpose in creation but only his subsequent purpose after the fall not only subordinates salvation to creation (since salvation becomes "plan B," something of an "embarrassment" to God), but it also implies that we do not know what sort of God it is with whom we have to do in creation. Thus theology begins with the mysterious God (*Deus absconditus*) of creation, whereas it should begin with the revealed God (*Deus revelatus*) of redemption. In other words, Barth argues, since God has revealed himself in Christ as Redeemer, theology should begin where God himself begins—namely, with his electing purpose in Christ. Technically referred to as Barth's "Christomonism" or "Christocentricity," this view permeates his whole theological vision. He holds that the church rests upon the eternal covenant in Christ, which is the inner ground of creation, and so on.[50]

---

49. When one peruses the infralapsarian literature, however, it is obvious that this inconsistency is *not* obvious to the infralapsarians. Hodge and Warfield, for example, seem quite oblivious to the problem. Note also how Article 7 of the Canons of Dort speaks as though the human race had fallen (the verb, *prolapso*, is a participle, "being fallen") before the world was created. For a brief defense of the infralapsarian position (one which, incidentally, illustrates its logical fallacy), see B. B. Warfield, *The Plan of Salvation* (Grand Rapids: William B. Eerdmans, 1942).

50. Note, for example, his statement that the man must have the woman to be complete *because* (German *weil*, not *also*) the man Jesus will not be alone but must have his church (*CD*, 3/1: 321).

And this church, the *regnum Christi*, does not merely stand alongside some other kingdom, says Barth. Rather, the height of the original creation and the depth of the sinful creation are embraced in that mighty decision of the God who acts in Jesus Christ. This is the God who not only acts but wills from all eternity to be this God, the God who chooses to be who he is in Jesus Christ: the Creator, Redeemer, and Sanctifier. Hence, God is from the beginning the God whose gracious purpose is served not only by creation but also by sin, death, the devil, and hell. Hence also, the election of grace belongs before creation, providence, and salvation (see *CD*, 2/2: 76 – 93).

Amyraut, by contrast, went so far in his rejection of Beza and others adopting his position as expressly to affirm that God did indeed change his mind after the fall: "And sin seems to have changed not only the whole face of the universe, but even the entire design of the first creation, and, if one may speak this way, seems to have induced God to adopt new counsels."[51] Thus, for Amyraut God becomes the God who declares the end not from the beginning but from the fall. He is the God who, as Barth would say, opts with some embarrassment for "plan B." (For a summary and critique of aspects of Amyraut's position, see pp. 101 – 2 herein.)

The supralapsarian, then, contends that although God carries out his purpose in a temporal sequence — beginning with creation, followed by the fall, and culminating in the salvation of the elect and condemnation of the reprobate — this order is reversed so far as his purpose is concerned. *Though all the means are prior to the end in time, they are subservient to it in thought.* That is to say, God's plan reflects a logical rather than a temporal order.

It is, to use an illustration, like when a young woman purposes to buy a gift for her fiancé's birthday. Pondering the matter, she resolves to purchase him a certain make of watch. Since this make of watch is available only through an importer in a neighboring city, she resolves to go to this city during her day off from school a week hence. In carrying out this plan, however, she reverses this order. The first thing she does — go to the city on her day off — is the last

---

51. Amyraut, "Brief Traitte de la predestination," quoted by B.G. Armstrong in *Calvinism and the Amyraut Heresy* (Madison: University of Wisconsin Press, 1969), p. 181.

thing she resolved to do; and the last thing she does — present the gift of the watch — is the first thing that she purposed.

This is only an analogy, to be sure, since the young woman not only carries out her plan in time (like God) but also makes the plan in time (unlike God). But the common element in the comparison is the fact that the young woman went to the city on a certain day because she purposed to give her fiancé a gift. The reverse would be illogical. We would not say that she purposed to give her fiancé a gift because she purchased a watch or that she purposed to purchase a watch because it was her first day off from school. Of course people sometimes act in this manner. Finding themselves with some free time, they go for a little ride, end up in a certain city, window shop, buy a watch, and then ask themselves what they will do with it. Such action, however, is not purposeful.[52]

But according to Scripture, God's action is always purposeful. He is the Lord of hosts who has sworn, "In very truth, as I have planned, so shall it be; as I designed, so shall it fall out" (Isa. 14:24, NEB). He does not make a world and then ask himself what he will do with it. He is the God who knows and declares the end from the beginning. Of course infralapsarians also insist — inconsistently — that the fall did not frustrate God's purpose, much less take him by surprise; they simply claim that it was not a part of his *original* purpose in creation.

Although we may state that the general purpose of God in creation is the manifestation of his glory, we cannot say how he would have achieved this end had humankind not fallen. Such a matter is simply an impenetrable mystery. But for the supralapsarian this mystery has been dispelled by the light of revelation. We do know what God had in mind when he purposed to create the world: the salvation of the elect and the condemnation of the reprobate. Supralapsarians appeal to such scriptures as Romans 9:11ff., which says that "God's purpose of election" is established (μενη) not only

---

[52]. On the nature of rational thought as logically the reverse of its fulfillment in time, see Aristotle's *Physics*, book 2, chap. 9, and the commentary of various scholars thereon. See also *The Ethics of Aristotle*, ed. John Burnet (1900; Saint Clair Shores, Mich.: Scholarly Press, 1976), chaps. 35–36. As I write, I have before me a cartoon showing the president of the United States standing before a Rube Goldberg contraption called an MX missile and saying, "First we make it and then we ask what it is and how we will use it."

in the choosing of Jacob apart from his having done good, but also in the rejecting of Esau apart from his having done evil. They also appeal to Ephesians 3:8–12, in which the apostle says,

> To me . . . this grace was given, to preach to the Gentiles the unsearchable riches of Christ, and to make all men see what is the plan of the mystery hidden for ages in God who created all things; that [ἵνα of purpose] through the church the manifold wisdom of God might be made known to the principalities and powers in the heavenly places. This was according to the eternal purpose which he has realized in Christ Jesus our Lord, in whom we have boldness and confidence of access through our faith in him.

In this passage, to be sure, Paul uses the ἵνα of purpose with reference to creation only, not with reference to the fall. Yet there is no need that he should mention the fall expressly, since he and his readers agreed that God did not create the world fallen and alienated; the fall is the creature's rather than the Creator's work. So, say the supralapsarians, in this passage it is obvious that the apostle is not speaking of some abstract, ideal world that might have been had humankind not sinned. And why is this so obvious? Because in an unfallen world there would have been no preaching "to the Gentiles of the unsearchable riches of Christ," nor would there have been a making known of God's wisdom through the church "according to the eternal purpose which he has realized *in Christ Jesus.*"

If we accept the apostle's statement, then, we cannot exclude the fall and our sinful history from the ultimate purpose of God in creation. In other words, in view of this text, one cannot say simply that God created in order that he might be glorified. To be true to what Paul says, one must say he created in order that he might be glorified *through the church*—that is, *through the salvation of his people from their sins*. And this implies that God is also glorified in the judgment of the wicked. We must not forget that the "hallelujahs" of Handel's *Messiah*, inspired by the thought that the "Lord God omnipotent reigneth," are preceded by another "Hallelujah!" inspired by the thought that God's "judgments are true and just" and that "the smoke from Babylon goes up for ever and ever" (Rev. 19:1–8).

And this is saying much more than that there would have been no fall had God not created the world, and that there would have been no salvation had there been no fall. This much is self-evident.

Rather, the question is how we are to construe these matters—creation, fall, redemption—when speaking of the divine purpose. The supralapsarians answer that since it is God's final purpose to display his manifold wisdom to all intelligent creatures through the church, the company of the redeemed, it must be his purpose that humankind should rebel and fall into sin in order that he might redeem some (the elect) and condemn others (the reprobate). And since he so purposed, he must further have purposed to create humankind and the world in which we live as the theater for the great drama of sin, salvation, and judgment.

Because the supralapsarian position is logically coherent, it has appealed to many theologians.[53] One might wonder, then, why it has never been accepted by the majority, even within the ranks of the Calvinists, nor adopted in any official creed or confession. We need not look far for the reason. To affirm that the fall of humankind is just as much a part of God's purpose as creation or salvation gives one pause, to say the least. To espouse the supralapsarian view, logical though it may be, is not only to say that the devil is "God's devil" (as Luther says, and indeed as everyone who is not a metaphysical dualist must say), but it is also to say that the devil is God's devil *just as much* as Jesus is his Christ, and that the fall into sin is *just as much* God's work as is salvation from sin.

The doctors at the Council of Trent minced no words on this latter point: "If anyone says that it is not in man's power to make his ways evil, but that the works that are evil God works as well as those that are good, not permissively only, but properly, and of himself, in such wise that the treason of Judas is no less God's own proper work than the vocation of Paul: let him be anathema" (Canon 6, "On Justification." On Barth's attempt to escape the Tridentine anathema by suggesting that Judas was as much an apostle as Paul, albeit a "negative" one, see pp. 53–54 herein.)

By the same token and for the same reason, Barth speaks of the fall as necessary with an eternal and absolute necessity. Describing Satan and his kingdom as the shadow of the light of Jesus Christ's election, he affirms that this shadow is the *necessary* object of rejection in the divine counsel.

---

53. It has in fact appealed not only to Zwingli, Calvin, and Beza in the Reformed tradition, but also to Luther. Of course none of the Reformers thought in terms of the lapsarian controversy of the seventeenth century specifically, much less did they consistently work out the implications. Zwingli's *De Providentia*, however, is a piece of rigorous logical thought beginning with the premise that God's power is *potentia absoluta* and thus it anticipates the subsequent controversy.

(Where there is light, it seems, there must be a shadow, not only in physics but also in theology.) The reality of this shadow is grounded in the divine will, he says, and testimony is given to it by the fall of humankind, an event that fulfills this will.

> When confronted by Satan and his kingdom, man in himself and as such has in creaturely freedom no power to reject that which in His divine freedom God rejects. Face to face with temptation he cannot maintain the goodness of his creation in the divine image and fore-ordination to the divine likeness. (*CD*, 2/2: 122)

We have heard of the moral impeccability of the second Adam, but here we appear to have the immoral impeccability of the first Adam! Barth proceeds from his contention that the first Adam could not make it in the face of temptation to contend that *we*, as fallen in him, cannot make it in the face of similar temptation. Thus, by a kind of sleight of pen, the *non posse non peccare* (to use Augustine's terminology) of the alienated creation becomes the description of the original creation. Hardly the best page in Barth's *Dogmatics*!

The final inference of the supralapsarian view would seem to be that ultimately hell is just as much a part of the Creator's purpose as heaven. The majority have found this (and all the other conclusions mentioned above) intolerable. True, the Bible speaks of a hell "prepared for the devil and his angels" (Matt. 25:41) and of a "second death" (Rev. 20:6, 14; 21:8)—that is, a death after which there is no more a possibility of life. But the final word is, "Behold I make all things new" (Rev. 21:5). There is nothing new, however, in death and hell. The seer speaks of seeing "a new heaven and a new earth" (Rev. 21:1–22:5), but the lake that burns with fire (21:8) is not new. In whatever way hell is hell, it surely is not hell in the same way that heaven is heaven. Heaven is heaven because God dwells there—"He will dwell with them, and they shall be his people" (Rev. 21:3). Hell, by contrast, is hell because God does *not* dwell there, and those who do are not his people. The god of hell is the Devil, and its inhabitants are his minions.

The long and short of the matter is that supralapsarianism, so attractive for its inner coherence, is yet intolerable for its ethical implications. True, ethical judgments are not of the same sort as rational judgments. But when it comes to the subject of theology, they are just as weighty, if not more so. We cannot subscribe to a view of predestination that would be tantamount to making God deny himself.[54] Such, of course, is by no means the intent of supralapsarians. But their view does leave one wondering whether the effort to "understand," the desire to "explain" the doctrine of predestination, to press the logical implications of the divine sovereignty, has not in the end led to the same impasse for which we faulted the Eastern and Arminian view. Is it not possible that both views, each in its own way, is incompatible with Scripture?

To be sure, there is a great gulf fixed between the two positions. And if one were to appeal to Scripture, surely the freedom (sovereignty) of God is a more fundamental truth than the freedom (responsibility) of the creature. As we have noted, human freedom is grounded in the divine freedom, not vice versa. But the divine freedom is not arbitrary; it is grounded in God himself, the God who is the "I AM WHO I AM" (Exod. 3:14). However, a doctrine of predestination that makes all that happens God's work in the sense that the shadow is as necessary to the light as the light is to the shadow (to borrow Barth's figure) is quite another matter. Given such a view, human freedom is not so much grounded in the divine freedom as swallowed up by it. And what becomes of the God who not only loves his people, but *is* love in himself (1 John 4:16)? Would a God who creates in order to condemn be the God who is who he says he is — that is, the God that swears by himself, "As I live . . . I have no pleasure in the death of the wicked, but that the wicked turn from his way and live" (Ezek. 33:11)?

It is worthy of note in this regard that Berkouwer begins his volume *Divine Election* with a chapter entitled "The Boundaries of Reflection." In it he ruminates on Bullinger's hesitance (in contrast to Zwingli, Luther, and Calvin) to include the fall among the events occasioned by the divine will. If judgment is the act of God *against* the sinner for his sin, how, asks Bullinger, can God have predestinated the sinner to sin? Would this not threaten to make God the author of sin (*autor peccati*)? This, of course, has been the charge

---

54. Having elaborated the doctrine of predestination in great detail, the subscribers of the Canons of Dort conclude by repudiating the thought that God "by a mere arbitrary act of his will has predestined the greatest part of the world to damnation, and has created them for this very purpose; that *in the same manner* in which election is the fountain and cause of faith and good works, reprobation is the cause of unbelief and impiety" (Schaff, *The Evangelical Protestant Creeds*, p. 596).

of the opponents of double predestination from the beginning, a charge that Calvin repudiated and Arminius reiterated. It is, of all the "hard sayings" associated with the name of Maccovius and other supralapsarians at Dort, the hardest and the one that none has ever been willing to make. But there are other hard sayings that some *have* been willing to make—such as, for example, Calvin's reference to the *"decretum horribile."*

Generally these hard sayings are found on the lips of the opponents of predestination who seek thereby to discredit the doctrine. But sometimes they are also spoken by its adherents. This is because they accept the hermeneutical principle that things necessary for God's glory and our salvation are not only "expressly set down in Scripture but by good and necessary consequence may be deduced from Scripture" (Westminster Confession, chap. 1, sect. 6). One can hardly fault this hermeneutical canon, for even the doctrine of the Trinity is only an inference from Scripture—yet, as the church has generally agreed, "a good and necessary one." However, the doctrine of the Trinity, it must be remembered, though it rests on inference, does not seek to eliminate the mystery of God's being by explaining how God could be three in one. It rather guards than explains the mystery. By contrast, some of the implications drawn from predestination seem to attempt an explanation of what in the end simply cannot be explained. In any case, inference is the language of logic and system, and system building can easily lure one into speculation that goes beyond the animus of revelation.

The doctrine of the fall confronts us with further mystery: on the one hand it is an act of rebellion against the will of God, but on the other it is not outside the will of God. But can we bring these two affirmations together logically? Can we—should we—seek to explain this paradox? It would seem that the supralapsarian explanation leads us to intolerable results in the extent to which it compromises what Scripture teaches concerning the nature of God as Love. The high doctrine of supralapsarianism, in other words, contradicts Scripture in a covert way, even as Arminianism contradicts it in an overt way.[55]

---

55. This is not the case with respect to Barth's restatement of the doctrine, of course, since *apokatastasis* is as overt a contradiction of the Scripture as Arminianism. It is to Barth's credit that he recognized this and never fully embraced the implications of his own position in this respect. And the same may be said, *mutatis mutandis*, for the Wesleyan Arminians and their doctrine of free will.

Stated precisely, the problem with supralapsarianism is the way it views reprobation. Given such a view, the light of electing grace is eclipsed by its own shadow, the "horrible" decree. The gospel is still heard in the supralapsarian message, but it is a letter edged in black. In Scripture election is always deemed a blessing: "Blessed is he whom thou dost choose and bring near, to dwell in thy courts" (Ps. 65:4). We should not state the doctrine of the divine rejection implied in this choice so as to rob us of this blessing. We should not allow our effort to "understand" the place of sin in the divine purpose to lead us to the conclusion that where grace abounded, sin did much more abound.

We conclude, then, that the supralapsarian view is most attractive for its inner coherence. It not only treats the doctrine of election and reprobation *sub specie aeternitatis* but does so with such consistency that the divine choice (sovereignty) is fully affirmed both in the grace of election and in the severity of reprobation. Here, indeed, "God's purpose of election" is made to stand, not only in the case of Jacob, who is loved, but also in the case of Esau, who is hated. *However, this logical symmetry is obtained at too great a price.* As the elect are created to be "vessels of mercy," so the reprobate are created to be "vessels of wrath." How can this be? If the Holy One revealed in Scripture is Love, how can he be the God who predestines his creatures to sin in order that he might condemn them?

Faced with this question, the great majority, even in the Reformed tradition, have backed away from the supralapsarian position and settled for a less coherent approach. This latter view, technically known as infralapsarianism, is tacitly or explicitly found in all the major confessional statements coming out of the Reformation. In the Reformed tradition especially, these confessions affirm again and again that while God chooses the elect without consideration of their merit, the reprobate are by contrast left in their sins and on the basis of those sins justly condemned. There is no effort to set aside the asymmetry in Augustine's doctrine of double predestination, even though it has troubled the theologians. Indeed, this asymmetry is rather affirmed. The great adversative of Romans 6:23—God's gift is eternal life, *but* sin's wage is eternal death—is clearly heard. The great contrast between the gift of life (election) and sin's awful wage (reprobation) is fully maintained. As the Canons of Dort affirm (in the "First Head of Doctrine"), though the reprobate are predestined in the sense that they "are passed by in the eternal decree," "this decree is 'irreprehensible' because it is the divine resolve to leave [them] in the common misery into which they had willfully plunged themselves" (Art. 15). Hence, this "decree of reprobation by no means makes God the author of sin (the very thought of which is blasphemy)" (Art. 15), inasmuch as "the cause or guilt of this unbelief, as well as of all other sins, is *nowise* in God, but in man himself" (Art. 5). Obviously, such statements relieve the ethical problem that besets the supralapsarian position, and there can be no doubt that that is what they were intended to do. While there is unconditional election, there is no unconditional reprobation.[56]

The first major defense of the infralapsarian view (though the term itself is not used) is found in Zanchius's statement of the doctrine of predestination, which was originally part of a Declaration of Faith given before the Strassburgh Senate in 1562, shortly before Calvin's death.[57] In this statement, Zanchius affirms nine propositions in which he works through the problem of reprobation along infralapsarian lines.[58] He argues that God has determined both to leave the reprobate *in* their sins and to punish them *for* their sins. The former is "preterition" or "bare non-election" and is a purely negative matter; the latter is "condemnation," a positive appointment to punishment. The will of God is the reason of the former; the sins of the nonelect are the reason of the latter. God's not choosing some is "the fruit of his sovereign will, but his condemning them . . . is

---

56. Of course such statements do not constitute an *express* condemnation of supralapsarianism, since the reprobate as well as the elect are admittedly the objects of predestination; there is, however, a *tacit* condemnation in the refusal to draw out the logical implications of this double predestination. And this refusal, of course, means that the infralapsarians settle for a rational contradiction. In this regard, note Harry Boer's allusion to the "profound self-contradiction" in which Dort is involved (*The Doctrine of Reprobation in the Christian Reformed Church* [Grand Rapids: William B. Eerdmans, 1983], p. 20; this study came to my attention only after the above was written).

57. The best-known statement of infralapsarianism is probably that of Turretin, in Question 9: "Concerning the Object of Predestination," in his *Institutio* (Geneva, 1688; reproduced in *Reformed Dogmatics*, ed. J. W. Beardslee III, Library of Protestant Thought [New York: Oxford, 1965], pp. 361ff.). Our discussion will draw on Zanchius rather than Turretin, however, since the latter's statement of the argument is obviously an inferior piece of workmanship.

58. See Zanchius, "Of Reprobation or Predestination as It Respects the Ungodly," chap. 4 of Zanchius's *Absolute Predestination*, trans. Augustus Toplady (rpt; Evansville: Sovereign Grace Book Club, 1960).

the fruit (not of their non-election, which was no fault of theirs, but) of their own positive transgression."[59] "God is the Creator of the wicked, but not of their wickedness; he is the author of their being, but not the infuser of their sins."[60] Nor is God a respecter of persons, argues Zanchius, for it is out of the mass of fallen humanity, all of which is worthy of condemnation, that he vouchsafed to save some. Nor, again, is God's decision to punish the reprobate unjust, he says, for they are freely inclined to the evil they do. He does not spur them on like a rider a reluctant horse, compelling them to sin, but simply utters the tremendous word, "Let them alone."[61] According to Zanchius, then, the freedom of the reprobate is the ground of their responsibility.

The difficulty with this argument is that while it says less than the supralapsarians would say, in the last analysis it does not say anything essentially different from what they say. This becomes clear when one raises the thorny issue of the fall as it relates to the will of God. It is, in fact, at this point that the infralapsarian argument begins to unravel. Being double predestinarians, the infralapsarians cannot say that God simply *foresees* that the reprobate will fall and so become a part of the mass of fallen humanity. To argue thus would be to borrow a leaf from the Arminians' book.[62] To avoid postulating a reprobation based on mere prescience, therefore, they often say that God "decreed to permit" the fall. While they contend

---

59. Zanchius, *Absolute Predestination*, p. 125.

60. Zanchius, *Absolute Predestination*, p. 109.

61. Zanchius, *Absolute Predestination*, p. 111. One cannot but ask whether this is what Scripture says to Pharaoh: "For this purpose I have let you alone" (Rom. 9:17). Or again, "Jacob have I loved and Esau have I let alone" (Rom. 9:13).

62. Just how near the toils of the Arminian argument can come for the infralapsarian is seen in Zanchius's remark that the condemnation of the ungodly is not unjust because they are ordained to punishment "under that [ungodly] character alone" (*Absolute Predestination*, p. 109). One is reminded of the quaint argument of John Bunyan that since God infallibly foresees the impenitence of the reprobate, we may conclude that he will infallibly condemn them. "Did I infallibly see that this or that man would cut out his heart in the morning, I might infallibly determine his death before night." How true—and irrelevant! (See Bunyan's "Reprobation Asserted; or, The Doctrine of Eternal Election and Reprobation Promiscuously Handled," chap. 6 in *The Complete Works of John Bunyan*, ed. John P. Gulliver [Philadelphia: Bradley, Garretson & Co., 1873], p. 703. Not all authorities attribute this work to Bunyan.)

that it is for "adorable and unsearchable reasons" that he wills to permit the fall, they nonetheless concede that the fall is his will.[63]

Hence, we are not talking about "a bare negative permission" when we speak of the decree to permit the fall. Rather, the reprobate "from all eternity are positively ordained to continue in their natural blindness." But if we say the reprobate are what they are (i.e., morally and spiritually blind) by the positive ordination of God, are we not very close to the supralapsarian view? How close can be seen from Zanchius's fourth proposition:

> As the future faith and good works of the elect were not the cause of their being chosen, so neither were the future sins of the reprobate the cause of their being passed by; but both the choice of the former and the decretive omission of the latter were owing, merely and entirely, to the sovereign will and determining pleasure of God.[64]

And so in the end, it seems, there is no consistent position between a mere foreknowledge of the fall, which is Arminianism, and a foreordination of the fall, which (by implication at least) is supralapsarian. For this reason the pendulum of the infralapsarianism argument swings now to one side, now to the other. But when it comes to rest, it is much nearer the supralapsarian than the Arminian view. In fact, supra- and infralapsarianism are but nuances of one and the same fundamental approach. They both view not only election but also reprobation *sub specie aeternitatis*.[65] The for-

---

63. There are many variations on this theme. "God," says Zanchius, "permissively hardens the reprobate with an efficacious permission." But of all the strained formulas, none exceeds that of Toplady, who, as Zanchius's translator, affirms that God "preemptorily ordained to suffer the fall of Adam" (*Absolute Predestination*, p. 8n.1).

64. Zanchius, *Absolute Predestination*, pp. 108–9. Since according to Matthew 23:41 hellfire was prepared for the devil and his angels from eternity, Zanchius reasons that they must have been prepared for that fire from eternity (*Absolute Predestination*, p. 107).

65. It is, therefore, quite inaccurate and misleading to speak of supralapsarians as double predestinarians and infralapsarians as single predestinarians. What one should say is that the former are more concerned with the logical implications of the doctrine of predestination, and the latter are more concerned with its moral implications. Of course there have been many theologians from Augustine's day onward who simply refuse to say that God's will embraces the fall and the consequent sin of the reprobate, even by way of permission. But such are not representative of the infralapsarians. The implications of such a view, in fact, inescapably lead to Arminianism or, as in more recent times, to some form of the doctrine of a finite God.

mer, in its consistency, appeals to the mind; the latter, in its inconsistency, to the heart. Both can make impressive appeals to the Scripture, though in my own judgment the infralapsarians have the better of the argument in this respect. In any case, when all is said and done, the problem of reprobation remains unresolved and, it would appear, unresolvable.

3. The Divine Will as Antecedent and Consequent

Our conclusion that there is no satisfying solution to the problem of the divine will and human sin does not mean, of course, that no effort has been made to find one. How to get beyond mere prescience as the basis of election without ending up in some form of supralapsarian predestination is a challenge few theologians have been able to resist. Though it is hardly the most inspiring in the annals of theological endeavor, the story of this effort does afford the opportunity to see how certain theologians have tried to relate seemingly disparate strands of scriptural revelation—how they have sought to harmonize the affirmation that God wills the salvation of all (1 Tim. 2:4) with the affirmation that he hardens some according to his will (Rom. 9:18).

The early Eastern Fathers, for whom the rejection of Pelagianism by no means implied the acceptance of Augustine's doctrine of predestination, complained that Augustine's view of God's electing purpose as a hidden will did not do justice to his revealed will that all should be saved through the preaching of the gospel. Therefore they sought to clarify the issue by carefully defining the meaning of the term *will* when used of God. Eventually they sought to spell all ambiguity out of the phrase "the will of God" by distinguishing between God's will as antecedent and consequent (*voluntas Dei antecedens et consequens*). God's antecedent will is his general desire that all should be saved. It is the will revealed in the universal promise of salvation contained in the proclamation of the gospel. But this will assumes the readiness of sinners to repent and believe the good news that God in Christ is reconciled to them. What if they do not repent and believe? Then we must say that God does *not* will their salvation. When we so speak, we speak in terms of God's will as consequent—consequent, that is, upon the sinner's response to the gospel.

In this way, John of Damascus seeks to explain 1 Timothy 2:4: "God will have all men and women to be saved," when, as a matter of fact, not all are saved but only those who believe. The apostle is here speaking of God's antecedent will, says John.[66] Aquinas follows the Damascene in this distinction as he seeks to defend the thesis that the will of God is always fulfilled. He likens God to a just judge of whom we may say "that antecedently he wills all men to live; but consequently wills the murderer to be hanged. In the same way God antecedently wills all men to be saved, but consequently wills some to be damned, as his justice may exact."[67]

Many Roman Catholics, following Aquinas, teach that by an antecedent decree God wills the salvation of all and therefore he sent Christ to die for all. Yet, foreknowing the use, for good or ill, that each would make of the grace offered in Christ, he wills by a consequent decree the salvation of some only. Bavinck observes that Lutheran theologians, feeling that Dort condemned their views, likewise increasingly sought to resolve the problem of the divine will by assuming that the universal offer of the gospel reflects an antecedent act of the divine will that all *may* be saved, whereas the assurance that some shall infallibly *be* saved reflects a consequent act of the divine will based on foreseen faith in those who accept the gospel offer.[68]

Those in the Augustinian and Calvinistic tradition have not approached the problem in this way. Instead, they have held that God's will is always antecedent to, never consequent upon, the creature's will. At a deeper level, they have maintained that the effort to harmonize the universal and particular strands of Scripture by appealing to two divine wills introduces an intolerable dualism into the doctrine of God. "God's decree," observes Bavinck, "is the eternally active will of God: it is the will and purposing of God himself; . . . being God's will in action, it is one with his essence." It is his " 'immanent work,' determined by nothing else than by God himself."[69] Obviously, then, to speak of two wills of God in this context

---

66. See John of Damascus, *Of the Orthodox Faith*, 2, 29.
67. Aquinas, *Summa Theologica*, Q. 19, art. 6.
68. See Bavinck, *The Doctrine of God*, pp. 352, 355–56, 379.
69. Bavinck, *The Doctrine of God*, p. 370.

is to raise questions about the oneness of God and the unity of the divine purpose.[70]

This traditional concern with the oneness of God and his purpose has motivated Reformed theologians in more recent times to reject (as we have noted) the argument for a hidden, over against a revealed, will of God. There is no hidden God, since God has revealed himself in Jesus Christ, and God is who he has revealed himself to be. This concern to avoid a hidden God who is apart from Christ is behind Brunner's complaint that Augustine and those who follow him have separated election from Christ. Because of his understanding of Matthew 22:14—"many are called, but few are chosen"—Augustine argued that while God calls many through the proclamation of the gospel, only a few respond because only a few have been chosen in his secret will. Thus there is a mysterious will of God behind Christ—one might even say apart from Christ—a will that is other than the will revealed in the gospel. Such a position, it is argued, raises profound questions about the very character of God. Is there a hidden God of the eternal decree who is other than the God with whom we have to do in the gospel? Were this so, would we not have to do with two Gods?

It is true, of course, that the phrase "will of God" has a twofold sense in common usage. All Christians would say that it is God's will that we not steal, but it is not in this sense that they speak of his will when they say we should seek his will for our lives. In the former case, the term "will" is being used in the sense of a precept or commandment; in the latter case it is being used in the sense of a plan or purpose. In the former sense the will of God is plainly revealed (see Exod. 20:15) and need not be sought. In the

---

70. It was for this reason that the Westminster divines, after considerable debate, decided to use only the singular, "decree," when speaking of God's will of purpose (note the heading of chap. 3 of the Westminster Confession: "Of God's Eternal Decree").

The difficulty with Aquinas's appeal to the example of a judge who both wills the life of a person as a human being and the death of the same person as a murderer in order to illustrate the antecedent and consequent will of God is that God does not experience the creaturely finitude of the judge, who in such an instance is confronted with a tragic moral choice. The only way to make the analogy stick is to give the human will of the creature who sins against God the same status over against the divine will that the will of the murderer has over against the will of the judge. But when this is done, the Yes of the divine will of election can be checkmated by the human No of unbelief—and this is precisely what cannot happen, given an Augustinian approach to the doctrine of election. Witness, for example, the convolutions of Barth's argument at this juncture.

ELECTION AND PREDESTINATION

latter sense, however, it does need to be sought (see, e.g., Acts 9:6). Calvin employs this double usage, in some places speaking of the will of God's purpose as embracing all that happens in his providence and in other places speaking of the revealed will of God as that to which we should all yield a voluntary obedience. (The latter, according to Calvin, is the will mentioned in the third petition of the Lord's Prayer: "Thy will be done" [*Inst.*, 3, 20, 43].) Some Reformed theologians speak of God's will of "precept" or "command" as his will of "desire," since in the gospel God is said both to command and to plead with the sinner to repent.

But as helpful and necessary as such distinctions may be, they are of little worth in resolving the problem that the "universalistic" passages of Scripture pose for the predestinarian. Indeed, Calvin did not hesitate to say that God's will of command was, in the case of the reprobate, the means by which he fulfilled his eternal will of purpose to condemn them. When, for example, God bids Moses to tell Pharaoh "Let my people go!" this command is given in order that Pharaoh might thereby be hardened in his resistance and judged according to the divine purpose. Thus it is obvious that although Calvin speaks of the will of God in two senses, he is not doing so in order to resolve the problem before us. Calvin is not inclined to argue that God first wills the salvation of all and then later the condemnation of some; to the contrary, he maintains that God wills the salvation of some (the elect) and the condemnation of others (the reprobate) from eternity.

Yet we should also note that Calvin is not completely consistent in this regard. There are times when the sheer force of the text of Scripture constrains him to admit (albeit only ambiguously) that in some sense God "wills" the salvation of "all." Commenting, for example, on passages such as Ezekiel 18:23, in which God declares that he has no pleasure in the death of the wicked, Calvin refers to two meanings of the divine will:

> We hold, then, that God wills not the death of a sinner, since he calls all equally to repentance, and promises himself prepared to receive them if they only seriously repent. . . . Meanwhile, this will of God which he sets forth in his word does not prevent him from decreeing before the world was created what he would do with every individual.[71]

In his treatise on predestination, Calvin responds to Pighius that of course God is to be believed when, on his own oath, he declares that he wills not the death of the sinner but rather that the sinner convert and live. "But," he quickly adds,

> I contend that, as the prophet is exhorting to penitence, it is no wonder that he pronounces God willing that all be saved. But the

---

71. Calvin, *Commentaries on the First Twenty Chapters of Ezekiel*, 2 vols., trans. Thomas Myers (1849; Grand Rapids: William B. Eerdmans, 1948), 2: 247–48.

mutual relation between threats and promises shows such forms of speech to be conditional. . . . Now this is not contradictory of his secret counsel [will] by which he has determined to convert none but his elect.[72]

Reserved as Calvin is in such usage, some of his followers made a great deal of it. In fact, they used his reference to God's "willing that all be saved" in contrast to his "will" concerning the elect in rather creative ways, as we shall see in the following addendum.

First Addendum: A Comment on Amyrauldism

Moise Amyraut, a leading spokesman for the French Protestants in the seventeenth century, used Calvin's distinction between God's will of precept and his will of purpose in a novel way to solve the predestinarian problem.[73]

Rejecting the mainstream of seventeenth-century Calvinistic orthodoxy, Amyraut argues that the doctrine of election will prove a fatal labyrinth, as Calvin warns, if we begin by asking what God has decreed from before the foundation of the world. We must rather begin with what he has revealed to us in Christ. As a bit of pastoral advice, Amyraut's point is well taken. But his thesis is much more than pastoral. Beza and others, he claims, had become mired in the lapsarian controversy because they had emphasized God's "decretive" will and denied his "conditional" will, thus upsetting the balanced presentation of Calvin. This had forced them into arbitrary and dishonest exegesis of those Scriptures that teach the universal design and scope of the atonement.

The only way to repair this unfortunate development, according to Amyraut, is to ground the discussion of election in the doctrine of salvation rather than in the doctrine of God.[74] In order to

---

72. Calvin, *Concerning Eternal Predestination of God*, trans. and ed. J. K. S. Reid (London: J. Clarke, 1961), pp. 105–6; as quoted by Armstrong, *Calvinism and the Amyraut Controversy*, pp. 198–99.

73. See Armstrong, *Calvinism and the Amyraut Heresy*, for an exhaustive and sympathetic treatment of Amyraut's thought. The following summary of Amyraut's argument is largely drawn from this source, especially pp. 158–221, 267–68.

74. He reinforced this point by appealing to Calvin's placement of his material on election relative to the material on other topics in the final edition of the *Institutes*—not as a part of the first doctrine, God (theology), but between the doctrines of salvation (soteriology) and the church (ecclesiology).

do this, he contends, we must follow the order of the economy of redemption—that is, the order God himself has followed in the historical accomplishment of our salvation. And when we do, then God's conditional (antecedent) will (i.e., his will revealed in the work of Christ and the proclamation of the gospel) is seen to be primary. By the same token his absolute (consequent) will (i.e., his will revealed in the work of the Spirit in effectual calling) is seen to be secondary.

Having posited a twofold will of God in this unique sense, Amyraut goes on to construct a covenant theology that speaks of a conditional covenant (made with all) and an absolute covenant (made with the elect). The covenant of grace (*foedus gratiae*) is really the former, though it "includes" the latter. It is in this way Amyraut would eat his cake and have it too; it is in this way that he seeks to affirm both that God covenants to save all and that he covenants to save only the elect. However, he eschews the effort "to resolve the opposition of the two wills of God which seem so repugnant" on which these two covenants rest. Since both are revealed in Scripture, it would be wrong to slight one for the other in the interest of a rationally constructed, logically coherent theological system.

In spite of this protestation, he does seek, however, to resolve the problem. This effort at resolution leads him to adopt an economic view of the Trinity that verges on tritheism. The Father draws up the general plan of salvation for *all*; the Son carries it out for *all*; and the Spirit makes possible the fulfillment of the condition of faith in *some*. In other words, according to Amyraut, election is the work of the Spirit *rather than* the Father and the Son! In this way his *a posteriori* methodology leads to the merging of election with effectual calling. Rather than being a choice made before the foundation of the world, election becomes an event in history—namely, the moment of one's initial experience of salvation. And so once more we see how the treatment of election *sub specie temporis* ends up, willy-nilly, making the divine choice subservient to the human.

Second Addendum: Universal Language and the Property of Ambiguity

Because the effort to harmonize the universal statements in Scripture with the doctrine of election by appeal to God's antecedent and consequent will has proved unrewarding, many in the Augustinian and Calvinist tradition have taken a rather different approach, an approach that focuses on the ambiguity attaching to the language of quantity in those passages from the Bible that speak of God's will that *all* should be saved.

Elementary logic courses teach us that adjectives of quantity — *all, every, some, any* — are ambiguous. "All the angles of a triangle equal two right angles" and "all the angles of a triangle are less than two right angles" are both true statements if the word *all* is regarded collectively in the first instance and distributively in the second. Though theologians have been distrustful of the larger efforts of speculative reason, no one can escape such logical analysis at the elementary level. What follows, then, is a sort of illustrated exercise in simple logic.

We begin with the self-evident assumption that a sentence may be so ambiguous in itself that we will be able to determine its meaning only by considering its context. We know, for example, that when Luke says that on the day of Pentecost there were dwelling in Jerusalem Jews "from *every* nation under heaven" (Acts 2:5), he is speaking in the context of the first-century Jewish diaspora living throughout the Roman empire. As Gibbon reminds us, ancient authors, dazzled by the extensive sway and irresistible strength of the emperors, gradually came to confuse the Roman Empire with the entire globe. To use another example, when Paul writes to the Colossians that the gospel of which he was a minister "has been preached to *every* creature under heaven" (Col. 1:23), he speaks as a former Jewish rabbi for whom the saving knowledge of the true God had for centuries been the heritage of the Jewish people in a unique way. The radical new inclusivism that enabled him to say that in Christ there is neither Jew nor Greek (Gal. 3:28) also enabled him to speak of the unfettered proclamation of the gospel to the Gentiles in such inclusive terms. This was the context in which he spoke as the apostle to the Gentiles. The potential of this inclusivism has been more and more actualized through centuries of missionary effort, though it is still far from being literally true that the gospel has been preached to "every creature under heaven."

In a similar fashion, certain universalistic texts frequently cited in the election debate appear in contexts crucial to the adjudication of their meaning. It is only as we consider these texts in context that the ambiguity in the language of quantity they contain can be overcome. A text such as 1 Timothy 2:4 is a case in point. The affirmation that God "desires *all* men to be saved and to come to the knowledge of the truth" clearly depends upon a larger context—in this case the Pauline exhortation that his readers pray for all, specifically "kings and all who are in high positions," since such behavior is "acceptable in the sight of God our Savior, who desires all men to be saved." Since the first-century Christians were largely from the lower classes, many of them being slaves, this admonition to embrace the upper classes in their prayers is understandable. It is possible, then, to construe the text as focusing on the thought that God desires the salvation of all *classes*, a desire that will be fulfilled in the eschaton, when the Lamb is extolled as he who by his blood "didst ransom men for God from every tribe and tongue and people and nation" (Rev. 5:9).

Should one take the text in this way, it would correspond in meaning to Matthew 3:5, which declares that "Jerusalem and all Judea and all the region about the Jordan" went to hear John and to be baptized by him. This "all" is the all of class: it includes Pharisees and Sadducees (3:7) and, in Luke's account (3:10ff.), also tax collectors, soldiers, and the like. This also seems to be the meaning of "all" in John 12:32: "And I, when I am lifted up from the earth, will draw all men to myself." For surely when Christ is lifted up—that is, when the gospel of the cross is preached—all (literally) are not drawn to him. Indeed, it is only in the shadow of the cross that a Celsus becomes a true pagan, that Julian becomes an incorrigible apostate, that Nietzsche becomes a forerunner of Antichrist, that Stalin becomes a demonic tyrant.[75]

"All," then, does not necessarily mean "all" in the literal sense assumed by those who cite these Scriptures as proof texts. Even the frequently quoted word of Peter that "The Lord is not slow about his promise . . . but forbearing toward you, not wishing that any should perish, but that all should reach repentance" (2 Pet. 3:9) is ambiguous in itself. It need mean no more, in its immediate context, than that the Lord delays his coming not from negligent inatten-

---

75. Nietzsche's experience in the parsonage is well known. Concerning Stalin's distrust of the God "before whom he had bowed his head to the stone floor for eleven years of his youth," his growing up on the Old and New Testament, his expulsion from seminary, and so on, see Solzhenitsyn, *The First Circle* (New York: Harper, 1968), pp. 105, 114.

tiveness but out of longsuffering toward his people. He is not willing that any *of them* should perish, for, as Jesus says in another place, it is his Father's will that he lose none of all that he has given him (John 6:39). Were one to suppose such an interpretation, then the text of 2 Peter 3:9 expresses the thought of the familiar hymn:

> Bring near thy great salvation,
> Thou Lamb for sinners slain,
> *Fill up the roll of thine elect,*
> Then take thy power and reign.
> —*Alford*

Emmanuel will come, he will take his power and reign, when the full complement of his people has been redeemed from every tribe, tongue, people, and nation.[76]

Hence it would appear that many have read into certain universal texts more than is required. A recognition of the ambiguity in the language of quantity—"all," "every," "the world"—helps us, at least in certain instances, to relieve the paradox of a God who may be said to will both the salvation of all and the condemnation of some, a God who will have all to be saved (1 Tim. 2:4) while at the same time hardening whom he will (Rom. 9:18). Yet it is in certain instances only that such an approach offers help. We can only wonder at the sanguine confidence some theologians have shown in their efforts to reduce to a coherent system the larger paradox at the heart of the doctrine of grace. I do not share that confidence. Yet my sense of the inadequacy of logical analysis at this juncture does not, I believe, call into question the confidence that the church has placed in Scripture as a true and trustworthy revelation of God. Nor am I persuaded that nothing is to be learned from the long, arduous, and sometimes acrimonious effort of theologians to enlighten the difficult subject of divine election. I shall, therefore, make a few comments in my concluding section that I hope will point toward a resolution of the question.

---

76. In the same vein, note the popular gospel song (a favorite of my grandfather):

> On that bright and cloudless morning when the dead in Christ shall rise,
> And the glory of his resurrection share:
> When his chosen ones shall gather to their home beyond the skies,
> And the roll is called up yonder, I'll be there!
> —*Black*

ELECTION AND PREDESTINATION

SOME REFLECTIONS ON THE MYSTERY OF GRACE

To affirm both the sovereignty of the divine choice and the responsibility of the human choice in the matter of salvation is, in traditional usage, to affirm "the paradox of grace." My allusion at the close of the preceding section to "the larger paradox at the heart of the doctrine of grace" bears on an even more fundamental question—namely, the veiled character of revelation, the hiddenness of God even in his self-disclosure; the fact that God is the God whose thoughts are not our thoughts (Isa. 55:8), whose judgments are unsearchable, and whose ways are past finding out (Rom. 11:33).

To state this paradox in terms of our discussion is to ask how it can be that God hides the truth from the wise (Luke 10:21) while at the same time he stretches forth his hands to a disobedient and contrary people (Isa. 65:2; Rom. 10:21); how it can be that God swears by himself that he has no pleasure in the death of the wicked (Ezek. 33:11) while at the same time some of those wicked are vessels of his wrath fitted to destruction (Rom. 9:22). Though logical analysis may subdue Zeno's paradox of Achilles and the tortoise, can it subdue the paradox of a Savior who weeps over a city (Luke 19:41) that the Almighty laughs to scorn (Ps. 2:1–6; Acts 4:25–28)? Can logic tell us how our Lord could lament his rejection by the citizens of Jerusalem (Matt. 23:37) when it is by their rejection that he is made to drink the cup of death according to his Father's will (Matt. 26:39)? Can logic tell us how our Lord could exclude the world from his intercession (John 17:9) when his intercession is with the very God who gave his Son as an expression of his love for the selfsame sinful world (John 3:16)?[77]

---

77. Whether one understands the phrase ουτως γαρ ηγαπησεν ο θεος τον κοσμον in John 3:16 to mean "this is how much God loved the world" or "God loved the world so much," this at least is clear: the Son whom he gave in love and by whom all who believe have everlasting life is the Christ freely offered to all in the gospel. And the "all" in this latter instance loses its ambiguity when placed in the context of the historical narrative recorded in Acts. In the early mission of the church, Christ was offered to all alike, those who rejected him as well as those who accepted him.

While it is true that in the apostolic age he was not offered literally to all—Chinese, Mayas, Australian Aborigines—yet such were not excluded from the offer *because* they were Chinese, Mayas, or Australians; for in Christ there is neither Greek nor Jew, Barbarian, Scythian, Chinese, Mayan, or Aborigine, but Christ is all and in all (Col. 3:11).

This paradox of the divine mercy and judgment surely commends humility in those who would honor the data of revelation. It also strongly suggests that the truth in the ongoing debate over election is not all on one side. And as far as I am concerned, it further suggests that the resolution of the debate is not waiting to be discovered in some new permutation of the components of which the problem is made up. (Barth's architectonic efforts in this direction should tell us that.) Define terms as we will, refine arguments as we may (and theologians can), here, if ever, we see through a glass darkly. Yet we do see; the glass is not entirely opaque. While there are secret things that belong to the Lord our God, there are also things that have been revealed and therefore belong to us and to our children (Deut. 29:29). Among them is the truth of election. Indeed, election is a truth that belongs to us in a fundamental way. Says Schlatter,

> We proclaim the gift of God's grace in its entirety, the whole gospel, when we say: God has elected us. In election we have to do not only with a prerequisite of grace or with the initial states of grace, but with grace in its completeness and eternal glory. It is altogether God's gift that his eternal will should grasp us, bind us to himself, and make us the recipients of his love.[78]

As Barth has reminded us, salvation is the first, last, and central word of all dogmatics—for how else can we speak of God than as our Father, Savior, and Sanctifier? But election is the first, last, and central word of salvation (CD, 90–91).

We should not, then, waffle concerning the doctrine or hamstring it with a thousand qualifications or neutralize it with nicely balanced, artificially contrived compromises. The result of such an effort is not a doctrine—and surely not the scriptural doctrine of grace—but a committee report. We should rather confess that the God revealed in Scripture is the God whose grace is grounded in his free and sovereign choice of the sinner. As free and sovereign, this choice is antecedent to and independent of the sinner's choice. The sinner's choice, by contrast, is in no way antecedent to or independent of the divine choice; rather, it is grounded in that choice. God does not love us because we first loved him; rather, we love him because he first loved us (1 John 4:19). Hence, the ground of

---

78. Schlatter, *Das christliche Dogma*, p. 474.

the divine choice is a mystery that we can never fathom, since there is no necessity in God that he should love us, sinners that we are. And because God's choice is God's secret, we can never counter that choice with a *quo warranto*. Yet because it is God's choice, we may rest in the confidence that it is just, for "Shall not the Judge of all the earth do right?" (Gen. 18:25). "He cannot deny himself" (2 Tim. 2:13), for he is the "I AM WHO I AM" (Ex. 3:14).

To *confess* such a truth is not to *explain* it. Mystery confronts us on every side. Formal logic would suggest that where we have paradox, we have a screw loose in our argument. But there is a difference between paradoxes that result from fallacious argument and paradoxes that mark the limits of human thought. All rational thinkers have been compelled to recognize the seeming finality of paradox in this latter sense, the existence of the so-called *insolubilia*.[79]

Interestingly enough, such imponderables of formal thought have their counterpart in the objective world of empirical observation. When Barth, as a theologian, speaks of the "shadow side" of the doctrine of predestination, the figure he employs from the realm of light and shadow is reminiscent of the celebrated paradox in modern physics that light behaves sometimes as waves, sometimes as particles. Indeed, the dual character of light points to a deeper duality pervading all of nature in which subatomic particles, Maxwell's "imperishable foundation-stones of the universe," under certain circumstances shed their substance and become—*mirabile dictu*—undulating waves of energy. We live in what has been facetiously described as a universe of "wavicles"—that is, of waves that are particles and particles that are waves. Such a development in physics not only affords the theologian comfort but, in its own way, confirmation. Einstein once observed that "the deeply emotional conviction of the presence of a superior reasoning power, which is revealed in the *incomprehensible* universe, forms my idea of God."[80]

If the scientist finds the universe incomprehensible, who will wonder that the theologian finds the Creator of the universe incom-

---

79. It is in this sense that we use the word "mystery" in this discussion. By "mystery" we mean not only a truth inaccessible to human reason apart from revelation, the Pauline μυστηριον, but a truth hidden even in its revelation. The theologian's paradoxes arise out of the fact that God is hidden even in his revelation.

80. Einstein, as quoted by Lincoln Barnett in *The Universe and Dr. Einstein* (New York: Sloan, 1959), p. 106; italics mine.

prehensible? The observations with which I will conclude this study of the doctrine of election, then, are not intended to answer all questions, resolve all paradox, or remove all mystery. I agree with Berkouwer, who noted that "The way back is not the way of rational transparency. The knowledge of the electing God is not the outcome of rational considerations, but is found only when one walks in the way of truth."[81] Or, as Weber has observed, election is a truth grasped in experience, not in abstract speculation.[82] Yet experience includes thought, and therefore a few concluding thoughts about election and its counterpart, reprobation, are in order.

1. The Dynamic Relation of Eternity to Time

In the discussion to this point I have obviously favored the *sub specie aeternitatis* approach; I believe that the concept of divine election compels us to view our salvation from the perspective of eternity. While our salvation is an event in time, it is an event whose time is laden with eternity. This is the meaning of the "fore" in foreknowledge. We are elect according to the *fore*knowledge (*fore*ordination) of God the Father (εκλεκτοις...κατα προγνωσιν θεου πατρος, 1 Pet. 1:1–2). This is the meaning of the "pre" in predestination. As God's elect we have been *pre*destined (προωρισεν) to be conformed to the image of his Son (Rom. 8:29). We have been chosen in Christ before the foundation of the world (προ καταβολης κοσμου, Eph. 1:4). We are not only saved by grace, but it is a grace given us in Christ Jesus before times eternal (προ χρονων αιωνιων, 2 Tim. 1:9).

Whenever the Scriptures speak in this way, the subject is God; *he* is the one who *fore*ordains, who *pre*destinates, who chooses us and gives us his grace *before* the worlds were made. In my judgment, there is no way, then, to argue that election is an event in time, that election happens in our calling, that calling is the *structure* of our election. The only analogy that can be used, in the light of the data of Scripture, is one that likens God's election to a personal act of will at the human level, an act on his part that comes *prior to* and determines the subsequent event. An orphaned infant, to use an illustration, becomes a member of a family not only *because* its

---

81. Berkouwer, *Divine Election*, p. 329.
82. See Weber, *Grundlagen der Dogmatik*, 2: 505.

parents resolve to adopt it, but *after* they do so. Their resolve anticipates the infant's new status.

Yet this way of thinking about election, necessary though it is, is not without its problems, as the illustration makes clear. The orphaned infant made no decision; it simply became aware, in due time, of the decision that was made concerning it. Thus it has no responsibility in the matter.[83] But the Bible plainly says that the elect (in ordinary circumstances) *do* make a choice leading to salvation—indeed, *must* make such a decision—and that they are responsible for it. When the gospel is preached to them, they do not simply become aware that they are elect. Rather, they call upon the Lord for salvation; and this call is a free and responsible act.[84] Apart from this act there is no salvation and therefore no election (Rom. 10:13). How, then, can we speak of a prior divine decision, a decision made from eternity, that does not turn the human decision made in time into a simple recognition that one is elect (or reprobate), a mere awareness that does not have the quality of responsible decision?

As we have seen, traditional responses to this question have too often made eternity into a Procrustean bed that deprives time of the qualities of history. Some of the things Zwingli (and Luther) says, for example, appear to lock us into a determinism as rigorous as that of contemporary scientism. But when a question is difficult, it is always easier to fault an answer already given than to frame a new and better one. The truth of the matter is that we are unable to answer the question in a way that will commend a universal consent even among those who stand within the circle of faith and embrace the doctrine of grace. At this point, then, I would simply like to make some suggestions.

---

83. One might suppose that the problem would vanish were we to change the illustration from adoption of an infant to adoption of an adult—but then we would have no illustration. If God has chosen us before the foundation of the world, it is required in the illustration at the very least that the decision of the parents shall anticipate even the possibility of a decision on the part of the child.

84. Barth's claim that election is good news, the first word of the gospel, because the whole human race is elect in Christ, may be criticized as transposing the message of election into such a different key that preaching becomes simply the announcement of a *fait accompli*, the means by which sinners are made aware of their election. Having been told that they have the winning number, let them rejoice. If there be any *existenz* in the decision to which they are called, it is not "Get into the ark before the rain comes" (final judgment) but "Don't jump out of the ark (impossible possibility) because it has already rained" (judgment of Calvary).

ELECTION AND THE INDIVIDUAL

First, it might at least be helpful to remember that God's eternity is not a remote segment of our time. The "pre" of which we speak in *pre*destination is not the first point on a line that begins in a remote past and continues, in an unbroken sequence of causes and effects, down to the present. God does not choose us *before* we choose him in the sense that King David lived *before* Christ, and Luther *lived* after Christ. Yet most of us, even when we are trying to think precisely, tend to think in this way, conceiving of God's eternity as a piece of our time before our time began, a backward extension, as it were, of our time into an unending past.[85]

When we so temporalize eternity, we easily fall into the related error of tending to see all events in time as a series of causally determined effects, beginning with the will of God, which is the first cause. I will admit that the concept of the will of God as "first cause" has an impressive pedigree in theology, but it has become increasingly problematical as a conceptual model for the theologian. This difficulty is primarily the result of the impersonal character of the cause/effect relationships with which we are so familiar in the realm of scientific law. In this familiar realm, the primary meaning of cause has always been "that which [impersonal] brings about [deterministically] an effect that can be predicted." It is this impersonal determinism inherent in cause/effect relationships at the human level that makes it so difficult to transfer the concept of cause to divine/human relationships. It leaves no room for what Brunner has called "personal correspondence," the "I/thou" relationship between God and the human subject so fundamental to biblical revelation. A causal view of the matter explains why so many have construed predestination as implying a flat determinism.[86]

Furthermore, if we think of the divine will in election deterministically, there is always the danger that we will think of the effect

---

85. This misleading way of thinking of election as a decision made concerning us a long, long time ago is sometimes aided and abetted by the way Scripture is translated. Consider, for example, the unfortunate rendering in the RSV of προ χρονων αιωνιων in 2 Timothy 1:9 as "ages ago." The NEB's "From all eternity" is better.

86. Witness once more Wesley's sermon "Free Grace," in which he complains that if predestination is true, the elect will be saved with or without preaching and the reprobate damned with or without it. Hence the doctrine overturns the ordinance of God in that it makes not only the preaching of the preacher but also the hearing of the hearer so much vanity.

(salvation) unconditionally. But there is a divine condition (*conditionalis divinus*) to salvation—namely, "repentance toward God and faith in our Lord Jesus Christ" (Acts 20:21). Not just the individual who is elect, but "he who *believes* in him is not condemned"; similarly, "he who does not believe is condemned already," not because the individual is reprobate but "because he has not believed in the name of the only Son of God" (John 3:18).[87] Since Scripture speaks of faith in Christ as the condition of salvation—"believe in the Lord Jesus, and you will be saved" (Acts 16:31)—no doctrine of election, when properly stated, will suppress the genuine significance, the *existenz*, of the human decision.[88]

Therefore, rather than relate the divine choice and the human as cause and effect on a time line, we should relate them dialectically, that is, in terms of their dynamic inner tension and fruitful interplay. Such an effort to substitute a personal model for an impersonal, causal model does not imply a dualism, as though God's eternity and our time are two tracks that never meet. Rather, God's eternity gives meaning to our time; our temporal reality is, as it

---

87. If those in the Reformed tradition insist on the "divine condition" of *salvation*, as obviously they do, why, it might be asked, do they speak of "*unconditional* election"? The answer has been given that election is not conditioned on any foreseen merit in the sinner—that is, faith is not the *condition* but the *gift* of grace. The grace of salvation secures—if we might so speak—the condition of salvation. One is not saved *on the ground* of one's faith but, as the apostle says, "by grace *through* faith," which is itself the gift of God, not of works, lest anyone should boast (Eph. 2:8–9).

88. It seems to have been the intent of Bullinger to escape the consequences of Zwingli's causal approach to predestination (which does threaten the *existenz* of human decision) when he alludes to "the temptation in regard to predestination, than which there is scarcely any other more dangerous." He proceeds to elaborate on what this dangerous temptation is, saying,

> We do not approve of the impious speeches of some who say, "Few are chosen, and since I do not know whether I am among the number of the few, I will enjoy myself." Others say, "If I am predestinated and elected by God, nothing can hinder me from salvation, which is already certainly appointed for me, no matter what I do. But if I am in the number of the reprobate, no faith or repentance will help me, since the decree of God cannot be changed. Therefore all doctrines and admonitions are useless." (*Second Helvetic*, chap. 10, "Of the Predestination of God and the Election of the Saints")

Bullinger then suggests that such sentiments are contradicted by the words of the apostle and the proclamation of the gospel, which is preached for the very reason that it may be *believed*. We must heed the Lord's call, "*Come* unto me"; we must hear the assurance that "whosoever *believes* in him shall not perish."

were, enfolded in his eternity—and it is precisely that that gives our time, and the choice we make in time, genuine significance. Our choice has meaning not in spite of, but because of, the divine choice. It is because of the divine choice in eternity that our choice in time does not run shallow, that our faith in Christ becomes a matter of life and death, of heaven and hell. Thus, on the one hand we avoid the superficial optimism that we are the masters of our own fate and, on the other, the bitter resignation arising from the conviction that we are mastered by our fate. The concept of election as it is presented in Scripture is not some abstract idea suspended in an eternal realm apart from time; rather, the eternal choice gives transcendence to the temporal choice, making the moment of calling a moment "laden with eternity" for the sinner. It is election that makes the act of faith an act that participates in eternity.

Given such a dynamic relationship of eternity and time, the "pre" in predestination and the "fore" in foreordination underscore the truth that while God's saving activity is *in* history, yet it *transcends* history and so escapes the contingency of all that is mere history. Rather than reducing the human act of faith to an illusion, it assures us that our faith can never become an illusion. The news that we are chosen in Christ before the foundation of the world is good news because it means that our human choice is taken up into the divine choice and thus escapes the contingent nature of all plans, deliberations, and choices that are merely human. Our faith in Christ is not among those "best laid plans of mice and men" that will come to naught. The "antecedent" element, then, in the doctrine of electing grace is not so much chronological as dimensional: election does not foreclose human *freedom* but rather human *merit*; it does not relieve us of responsibility but of the need to achieve salvation by our own works, which are bound to fail.

At this juncture we should note that while election (eternity) and faith (time) are never merged in Scripture, neither are they severed. We can see this in Romans 8:28– 30, a passage in which Paul indicates that those whom God foreknew—or "chose beforehand," as Arndt and Gingrich have it[89]—he also predestinated, and

---

89. Προγινωσκω = "choose beforehand" (see Bauer, *A Greek-English Lexicon of the New Testament and Other Early Christian Literature*, trans. W. F. Arndt and F. W. Gingrich, 4th ed. [Chicago: University of Chicago Press, 1957], p. 710).

those whom he predestinated he also called, justified, and glorified. Thus the apostle links eternity to time in such a way that we are compelled to take the eternal and temporal parts of the sequence together. We cannot treat them as separate entities. Because Paul thought in terms of reciprocity between God's eternal and temporal works, he never seems to reflect the problem so often felt in later theological disputes—that is, he never gives the former (eternal predestination) that independent status that reduces the latter (the historical events of calling and justification) to meaninglessness. Nor, on the other hand, does he view the latter as having an autonomous status that could frustrate the former and compel God to adopt "plan B." Those whom he calls and justifies are those whom he has predestinated.

Finally, the order of the apostle's statement should be noted. While he links the eternal to the temporal, he begins with the eternal and moves to the temporal. And this order is theologically significant. The events of salvation history are what they are because they are based upon God's predestination. He does not predestinate those who respond to his call; he calls those whom he chooses and predestinates. (Here the Arminian position reverses the argument.)

Of course, this view of the dynamic (as opposed to the chronological) relation of time to eternity is not without its limitations. For example, there is no getting around the fact that there is a clear temporal reference implicit in the "pre" of predestination. The "προ" of προοριζω, προγινωσκω means "before," not "above" or "below." Thus, when the Scriptures say that God chose us in Christ "before" the foundation of the world, we cannot deny the temporal element in this way of speaking. This is why I am not suggesting that thinking in terms of the dynamic relation between the divine choice in eternity and the human choice in history is anything more than a *helpful* means of approaching the issue; surely I do not mean to suggest that the approach resolves all problems or answers all questions.

The time/eternity dialectic pervades all theology. This is especially apparent in the case of the doctrine of the Incarnation, for instance, which is at the heart of the Christian faith. The numerous explanations of the paradox that the eternal Word became flesh and thereby entered our time often seek to explain so much that they end up explaining away the truth. From ancient Adoptionism to modern Christologies-from-below, the truth preserved in the Chalcedonian formula *vere Dei, vere homo,* is threatened by the endeavor to understand the paradox in terms of rational thought. And the same may be said of the efforts to harmonize the concepts of God's eternal election and our free choice. By substituting rationally congruent argument for paradox, these efforts lose the truth by explaining it away. We do better, in both instances, to embrace the paradox and recognize the absolute uniqueness of that *"decisive* event" in which the eternal Son assumed our humanity and also the uniqueness of its counterpart, the *"deciding* event," in which the eternal Spirit calls us according to God's electing purpose. As the former is the turning point of human history, so the latter is the turning point of our individual history. Such radical events are not susceptible of final explanation, because they transcend the cause/effect realm of rational thought. Hence, they are truths about which we can speak only in paradoxes.

2. The Universal in the Particular

It is my contention that election is a truth that we should confess rather than explain; still, inasmuch as confession involves thought, I have ventured to make suggestions as to how we might find decisive significance in the sinner's choice of the Savior in the light of God's eternal choice of the sinner, arguing for a dynamic relationship between the two. Another matter that is only a little less difficult concerns the particularism and universalism of Scripture. We have noted that by definition election of some implies rejection of others. Yet the Scripture speaks of a God who loves the *world* (John 3:16), who sends his Son to be the propitiation for the sins of the *world* (1 John 2:2), and who commissions his apostles to preach the gospel to *every* creature (Mark 16:15). We have already reviewed various theological efforts to relieve this paradox, some more and some less plausible. We need only make a few final observations, which may be helpful, again not in resolving the paradox, but in our understanding of it.

Since Schleiermacher, many Protestant theologians have taken the universal strand of revelation as normative, to the exclusion of the particular.[90] Such theologians assume that the family of God is

---

90. Of course restitutionism (αποκαταστασις) of some sort has found a marginal place in the Christian tradition since Origen (A.D. 250). But in modern times it has moved much more toward the center as a truth widely agreed upon, and this modern approach is rooted in Schleiermacher's quest for the religion in the religions.

coterminous with the human race and thus that all will be restored in due time to fellowship with him as citizens of his kingdom.

Such a vision has an obvious attraction, but just as obviously it contradicts those scriptures that plainly teach the double issue of *Heilsgeschichte*. We read in no uncertain terms that there are both those who are on the right hand of the Judge on the last day and those who are on the left (Matt. 25:31–46), those who are vessels of mercy and those who are vessels of wrath (Rom. 9:22–23), those for whom Christ is the "cornerstone chosen and precious" and those for whom he is the stone of stumbling and rock of offense (1 Pet. 2:6–8), those who look for his coming as a blessed hope (Titus 2:13) and those for whom his coming will mean everlasting destruction because they know not God nor obey the gospel of our Lord Jesus Christ (2 Thess. 1:6–10). While some cry, "Amen. Come, Lord Jesus" (Rev. 22:20), others cry to the rocks and mountains, "Fall on us and hide us from the face of him who is seated on the throne, and from the wrath of the Lamb" (Rev. 6:16).

Such clear scriptural statements make a subscription to restitutionism quite unthinkable for one who accepts the authority of Scripture. To embrace such universalism would disavow the divine condition of salvation that as sinners we repent and believe in Christ (Acts 20:21) just as radically, in its own way, as would advocating the most extreme supralapsarianism. There would be no possibility that one should be finally lost, and therefore no deadly danger to the soul. The warning of Scripture to seek the Lord while he may be found, to call on him while he is near (Isa. 55:6) would become a pedagogical bluff. If supralapsarianism appears to make the human choice unreal, *apokatastasis* makes it palpably unnecessary. In the one case it is little more than an appearance; in the other, a superfluity.[91]

---

91. I speak here of the way matters appear to many—myself included. I readily acknowledge that both supralapsarian predestinarians and serious universalists sincerely believe and teach the need of repentance and faith. In the latter case, this "condition" of salvation is generally regarded as a human possibility apart from any encounter with, or even knowledge of, Jesus as the Christ. The former, then, are in my judgment more faithful to the distinctive claims of Christianity. One might say that a consistent liberal Protestant universalist would be inclined to read Romans 8:28, "All things work together for good"; an Arminian would read it, "All things work together for good to those who love God"; and a Calvinist would read it, "All things work together for good to those who love God, who are called according to his purpose."

ELECTION AND THE INDIVIDUAL

If supralapsarianism threatens the doctrine that God is Love by affirming that he created the reprobate to be damned (and that unconditionally), universalism threatens the doctrine that he is the Holy One by affirming that in the end all will reap life no matter what they sow, that none of our sins will in the end find us out, that wheat and tares alike will be gathered into the barn. To be faithful to Scripture and the God of Scripture, the Holy One who is Love, we must affirm *both* the particular and the universal strands of Scripture as expressions of his will. But again the question is how we are to do so.

In searching for an answer, we will do well to remember that election has a corporate as well as an individual aspect. In fact, we began our exposition of the doctrine with comments on corporate election—that is, on the election of the people of God. Too often in their efforts to untangle the complexities attaching to the question of individual election, theologians have lost sight of the corporate aspect of the doctrine. This is unfortunate, since the corporate aspect of the doctrine implies that the universal strand of biblical revelation is best understood as a promise that a new humanity is to be created through Israel and the church. From this corporate perspective, the doctrine of election does not stand in contradiction to the universal strand of revelation, because election itself is ultimately concerned with a universal community, the people of God.

For all practical purposes, the doctrine of election is first revealed in the call of Abraham and Sarah out of Ur of the Chaldees, and they are called not as individuals but as the father and mother of the nation of Israel. To that end they are assured of a seed as numerous as the stars of heaven and the sand on the shores of the sea (Gen. 22:17); and through this seed all nations of the earth shall be blessed (Gen. 12:3; Gal. 3:8). Hence Abraham is called the father of many nations (Gen. 17:5; Rom. 4:17). In fact, he is promised that he and his descendants through Sarah shall inherit the *world*— through the righteousness of faith (Rom. 4:13). It would of course be ridiculous to assume that we are meant to take this language literally, but this does not mean that we should therefore dismiss it as hopeless hyperbole. In fact it is a promise fulfilled in the coming of the Seed *par excellence*, the Messiah, who commissioned the apostles to make disciples of *all* nations (Matt. 28:19). Thus we see the contour of biblical universalism as it moves from the patriarchs and matriarchs to the nation of Israel and finally to the nations of all the earth.

And so election, which from the beginning is individual in Abraham and Sarah, is at the same time corporate and universal in their seed. The patriarchs and matriarchs are not individuals as such but the forebears of the chosen people, Israel. And from this people there arises the new humanity, the church of the living God, made up of both Jew and Gentile, the "middle wall of partition" having been broken down (Eph. 2:14). Hence the church can describe itself as

> Elect from every nation, yet one o'er all the earth,
>   Her charter of salvation, one Lord, one faith, one birth;
> One holy Name she blesses, partakes one holy food,
>   And to one hope she presses, with every grace endued.
>   —*Stone*

And from this "new creation by water and the Word," there eventuates a whole new cosmic order (οικονομια) in which God shall make all things new, "a new heaven and a new earth" wherein dwells righteousness (Rev. 21:5). In the realization of this hope—when many shall come from the East and the West to sit at table with Abraham, Isaac, and Jacob, with Sarah, Rebecca, and Rachel in the kingdom (Matt. 8:11)—God's universal, electing purpose shall be fulfilled. Then shall come the "restitution (αποκαταστασις) of all things" of which Peter spoke (Acts 3:21) on the day of Pentecost, when the church was born.

To be sure, this restitution does not take the form of the universalism advocated by many in our day. There are those who do not enter the gates of the city—dogs, sorcerers, fornicators, murderers, liars—whose names are not written in the Book of Life (Rev. 21:27; 22:15).[92] Hence, I do not understand the two occurrences of

---

92. Why this should be we cannot say, but in any case, we should not try to

> Snatch the scepter from his hand,
> Rejudge his justice,
> Be the God of God.
>   —*Watts*

There is the gift of God, eternal life; *but* there is also the wage of sin, which is death (Rom. 6:23). This awesome adversative is an emblem neither of the creature's power to frustrate God's electing purpose nor of a divine sadism that delights in the creature's misery. Rather, it is a warning that no one can say No to God with impunity. But who is sufficient for these things?

"all" (παντας ανθρωπους) in Romans 5:18 in a strictly parallel way, but rather in an analogous way.[93] To say with the apostle "As one man's trespass led to condemnation for all men, so one man's act of righteousness leads to acquittal and life for all men" is to speak in terms of the old and the new humanity. There is a natural humanity and there is a new (elect) humanity; the former is "in Adam," the latter, "in Christ." While they are not identical in number, yet this quantitative way of stating the analogy (cf. 1 Cor. 15:22, "as in Adam all die, so also in Christ shall all be made alive") does teach us to think corporately, holistically, when we speak of election.[94] To be chosen in Christ is to be made a member of his body, the church; and to be a member of the church is to look forward to the new creation already an inchoate reality in the church.

Election, then, is not an exclusivistic but a cosmic concept. It anticipates the time when, in response to the angel who preaches the everlasting gospel "to every nation and tribe and tongue and people" (Rev. 14:6), a new song shall be sung to him who has redeemed men and women from every tribe and tongue and people and nation (Rev. 5:9).[95] While the emphasis in this biblical universalism is on quality (the life of grace beyond the threat of death) rather than quantity (how many are saved), quantitative language is freely used in Scripture. For this reason it is appropriately found also in the devotion and worship of the church:

> From earth's wide bounds, from ocean's farthest coast,
> Through gates of pearl streams in the *countless* host,
> Singing to Father, Son, and Holy Ghost,
>   Alleluia, Alleluia.

—How

---

93. This in contrast to Joachim Jeremias, who insists that the πολλοι ("the many") of Romans 5:18 must have the widest possible breadth in both instances (*Theological Dictionary of the New Testament*, 10 vols., ed. Gerhard Kittel and Gerhard Friedrich, trans. Geoffrey W. Bromiley [Grand Rapids: William B. Eerdmans, 1964–76], 6: 542ff.; cf. H. N. Ridderbos, *Paul: An Outline of His Theology* [Grand Rapids: William B. Eerdmans, 1975], p. 341n.32).

94. "All" in Adam and "all" in Christ denote "all members of the class of persons belonging to them respectively" (Kümmel, as cited by Ridderbos in *Paul*, p. 341n.32).

95. The interpenetration of election and universalism—what might be called the election-in-universalism and the universalism-in-election—can be seen in this scripture. It is true the redeemed are from *every* (πασης) tribe; yet it is also true that they are *from* —that is, "out of" (εκ)— every tribe.

Even the avowed Calvinist Isaac Watts, moved by the "joy to the world" that One had come to rule "with truth and grace," sings,

> He comes to make his blessings flow
> *Far as the curse is found.*

The primary paradigm of this biblical universalism, as we have intimated, is the movement in redemptive history from the particularism of the Old Covenant to the universalism of the New. This universalism of the covenant as newly administered in Christ, in which the "dividing wall of hostility" is broken down, is the process whereby Jew and Gentile are made one in Christ, in order that "he might create in himself one new man in place of the two" (Eph. 2:13–15). This new humanity in Christ is the prototype of biblical universalism in its final, eschatological form.

Interestingly, in the opening chapter of Ephesians, the clear affirmation of election (particularism) is conjoined with an equally clear affirmation of its cosmic scope and purpose (universalism). Paul reflects on the fact that "we" (Jews who first hoped in Christ) and "you" (Gentiles who have now heard, believed, and been sealed by the Spirit) have both been predestined to live to the praise of God's glory. This is according to the purpose set forth in Christ "to unite all things in him, things in heaven and things on earth" (1:10). And so this union of Jew and Gentile in the church, of which Christ is the Head, harbingers the final rule of Christ over the *entire creation*.

This eschatological rule has already begun, as a matter of fact. It is inchoately realized in the exaltation of the risen Christ, who has had *all* things put under his feet. This exalted Christ has been made "head over all things for the church (και αυτον εδωκεν κεφαλην υπερ παντα τη εκκλησια), which is his body, the fullness of him who fills all in all" (Eph. 1:20–23). Thus is fulfilled the "mystery of his will" (v. 9) This mystery, revealed in Christ, is his eternal purpose to unite (ανακεφαλαιωσασθαι, literally "sum up," "bring everything together") all things in Christ (Eph. 1:10). The text does not say that all *are* the church, but that Christ's headship over all the creation is *for the sake* of the church. The creation achieves its true meaning in the church. And so the purpose of God in election embraces the entire created order.[96]

---

96. Traditionally theologians have suggested some sort of hierarchical structure at this point. Angels and the redeemed (the church), as subject to Christ, will

First Addendum: Election and the Question of Numbers

> Whosoever, therefore, in God's most providential ordering, are foreknown, predestinated, called, justified, glorified — I say not, even though not yet born again, but even though not yet born at all, are already children of God and absolutely cannot perish. . . . I speak thus of those who are predestinated to the kingdom of God, whose number is so certain that one can neither be added to them nor taken from them.[97]

The concept of the elect as a fixed number, so emphatically enunciated by Augustine at the beginning of the predestinarian debate, has become a standard part of the tradition.[98] There can be no doubt that Scripture often speaks in a way that suggests this approach. When the Lord says to Israel, "You only have I known of all the families of the earth" (Amos 3:2), the implication is plain: Israel, one nation among the many, and Israel only, is the object of his electing grace (see also Deut. 7:6). In the New Testament the objects of God's grace are also spoken of in terms of number. Israel's salvation is associated with the coming in of "the full number (πληρωμα) of the Gentiles" (Rom. 11:25); the martyrs of the Apocalypse are told that they should rest "until the number of their fellow servants . . . should be complete (πληροω) who were to be killed as they themselves had been" (Rev. 6:11).[99]

---

enjoy the highest degree of joyful union with him in the eschatological kingdom; the ungodly will be consciously subjugated to him; and the lower orders of creation — from the animal world to St. Francis's "brother sun and sister moon" — will be unconsciously subject to him.

97. Augustine, from his first sermon on sin and grace, as translated, with source, in R. C. Petry's *History of Christianity* (Englewood Cliffs, N.J.: Prentice-Hall, 1962), p. 111.

98. It was this part of the tradition, as we have already noted, that Barth rejected. According to Barth, the fatal mistake made by Augustine and those who followed him was to define the *numerus predestinatorum* as a distinct number of elect and reprobate individuals, a mistake he sought to "correct" by redefining that number as precisely one, Jesus Christ, the Elect Man who becomes the Reprobate Man. Others have criticized the concept of an exact number of the elect as too rigid and wooden, as an approach that entails a deterministic rather than a dynamic view of time and eternity. The thought that the predestinated are an exact number is found, however, not only in Christian but also in Jewish sources (see 1 Enoch 47:4; 2 Esdras 2:44).

99. It was commonly assumed in the Middle Ages that the number of the elect corresponded to the number of the fallen angels, whose decimated ranks were

The concept of a fixed number of the elect (*numeros electorum*) is implied also in the way in which the Scriptures speak of a Book of Life. Thomas devotes an entire section consisting of three Articles in the *Summa* (Q. 24) to the subject of the Book of Life. He understands it as an appropriate metaphor in speaking about predestination because it is usual for men and women who are chosen for a task (e.g., soldiers) to have their names inscribed in a book.[100] In the light of these Scriptures one can understand why the Westminster divines defined the universal church as consisting "of the whole number of the elect, that have been, are, or shall be gathered into one, under Christ the Head thereof."[101]

Interestingly, even when the circle narrows and Scripture speaks of the Remnant, the "Israel within Israel," this little band is defined numerically. There are, Elijah is told, seven thousand who have not bowed the knee to Baal (1 Kings 19:18; Rom. 11:4). While in its original context the largeness of the number seven thousand is intended to buoy up the melancholy spirit of the prophet, who felt that he was a minority of one, the very narrowing of the circle from one nation, small in itself, to a remnant within that nation, implies

---

thus replenished. Anselm assures Boso (*Cur Deus Homo*, chap. 16) that there is a reason why the number of the fallen angels must be made up from the ranks of the human race: "There is no question that intelligent nature . . . which was foreseen by God, was foreseen by him in a reasonable and complete number, so that there would be an unfitness of its being either less or greater." Boso obligingly expresses appreciation for such pearls of wisdom.

100. Translating Acts 13:48 as "all [believed] who had been enrolled for eternal life in the records of heaven," F. F. Bruce goes on to comment, "We cannot agree with those who attempt to tone down the predestinarian note of this phrase by rendering 'as many as were disposed to eternal life.' . . . The Greek participle is τεταγμένοι, from τάσσω, and there is papyrus evidence for this verb in the sense of 'inscribe' or 'enroll.' . . . The idea of being enrolled in the book of life or the like is found in several Biblical passages. . ., in the Jewish pseudepigrapha. . ., and in rabbinical literature" (*Commentary on the Book of Acts*, New International Commentary on the New Testament [Grand Rapids: William B. Eerdmans, 1968], p. 283n.72).

101. Westminster Confession, Chap. 25, "Of the Church." Though they have never speculated about the question of why the elect should be a certain number, those in the Reformed tradition have emphasized that the number is certain. Zanchius, for example, argued that if God knows the stars by name and numbers the hairs of our head, then he must know the number of the elect. To deny that the number is fixed and absolute, he suggests, would be to call into question God's immutability, foreknowledge, justice, and power (see *Absolute Predestination*, pp. 91–92).

that the number of the elect may not only be fixed, but few. This is the perspective reflected in the question put to Jesus as he journeyed toward Jerusalem: "Lord, will those who are saved be few?" (Luke 13:23). The answer is not a reproachful, "Of course not," but a sobering admonition: "Strive to enter by the narrow door; for many, I tell you, will seek to enter and will not be able" (v. 24).[102] Such an answer reminds one of the difficult saying of our Lord—"Many are called, but few are chosen" (Matt. 22:14)—a saying that has commonly been understood as implying that the number of the elect is small in comparison with the number to whom the gospel is preached.[103]

Even though the Bible ends with a vision in which John describes the company of the redeemed as "a great multitude which no one could number" (Rev. 7:9), the number of the wicked is described as being even more ominously large. When Satan goes forth to deceive the nations, those who follow him are said to be "like the sand of the sea," an army so vast that it completely surrounds "the camp of the saints." Obviously, the faithful in the beloved city owe their salvation not to their numerical superiority but to the power of the Almighty, who sends forth his fire from heaven to consume the enemy (Rev. 20:7–10).

There is, then, in Scripture a strand of revelation that accents the smallness of God's chosen people. One is reminded of Jesus' word, "Fear not, little flock, for it is your Father's good pleasure to give you the kingdom" (Luke 12:32).

Many in our day take umbrage at the suggestion that the elect are a small company. They cannot abide the thought, much less sing with Cowper,

> Dear Shepherd of thy chosen few,
>   Thy former mercies here renew;
> Here to our waiting hearts proclaim,

---

102. In the Matthean tradition similar materials are found in the Sermon on the Mount, in which citizens of the kingdom are described as those who enter by the narrow gate of life, which few find, in contrast to the broad way of destruction entered by the many (Matt. 7:13–14).

103. Brunner complains that it was Augustine's interpretation of this verse in terms of numbers that led to the faulty equating of the elect with a *certus numerus predestinatorum* (*Dogmatics*, 1: 341–42).

ELECTION AND PREDESTINATION

The sweetness of thy saving Name.[104]

They contend that such language gives the doctrine of election the tone of privileged elitism, that it cultivates a superior indifference to those who are not a part of the "in group."[105]

This business of pride is, indeed, a danger with the doctrine of election; clearly it can serve to foster a superiority complex. The opponents of the doctrine have often fixed upon this point—especially when it is a matter of Gentiles speaking of Jews, though the objection is a general one. Citing Arnold Toynbee, Baillie observes,

> More particularly, objection is taken to the Israelites' self-consciousness as being the Chosen People and to the claims of the early Christians to be the New Israel to whom the divine election has now passed. Dr. Toynbee has the severest possible things to say against such a conception. He speaks of the evil that is inherent in the belief that there is a "Chosen People" and that I and my fellow-tribesmen are It.

Baillie goes on to note Toynbee's prediction that curing half the human family of the presumption of exclusiveness that the doctrine of election fosters may well be the "most crucial episode in the next chapter of the history of mankind."[106]

I can only concur with the response Baillie makes to Toynbee and to those who share his sentiments. Election, Baillie reminds us, entails responsibility and service, not self-indulgent esteem. God did not (and does not) say to his people, "You only have I known of all the families of the

---

104. They would also balk at singing Watts's

We are a garden walled around,
    Chosen and made peculiar ground;
A little spot, enclosed by grace,
    Out of the world's wide wilderness.

105. Such a sentiment is vividly conveyed in the following anonymous parody:

We are the good Lord's chosen few;
There's room enough in hell for you.

Toplady cites the words of Henry IV of France on his birthday: "I was born on this day and, no doubt, taking the world through, thousands were born on the same day with me, yet out of all those thousands I am, perhaps, the only one whom God has made a king. How signally am I indebted to the particular bounty of his providence!" Toplady adds, "Similar are the reflections . . . of such persons as are favored with the sense of their election in Christ" (in Zanchius, *Absolute Predestination*, p. 18). Thus one person's arrogance is another's humility.

106. J. Baillie, *The Sense of the Presence of God* (New York: Scribners, 1962), p. 204. He is referring to Toynbee's *An Historical Approach to Religion*.

earth: congratulations!" Rather, he says, "You only have I known of all the families of the earth; therefore I will punish you for all your iniquities" (Amos 3:2). And the same is true of each individual who is numbered among his people. Hence, the right use of the doctrine of election leads not to pride but to humility. To say "Had Christ not chosen me, I would not have chosen him," is surely as humbling as to say "Had I not chosen Christ, he would not have chosen me." Spurgeon once observed that he was sure God had chosen him before he was born, for he never would have afterward.[107]

Peter, who calls the church "a chosen race," God's own people, also reminds us that once we were no people. Why then are we now God's people? Simply because we have received mercy (1 Pet. 2:9–10). Berkouwer entitles the last chapter of his volume on election "The Great Misconception." In it he observes that the danger of human pretentiousness lurking in the word *election* can be overcome only if we remember that election is God's *gracious* act. In other words, rightly understood, election is the cornerstone of the doctrine of *sola gratia*: it teaches us that our salvation is by grace alone. In addition we might note that election is God's *impartial* act. The electing God is no respecter of persons (Acts 10:34; Rom. 2:11; 1 Pet. 1:17): he chooses his people not for anything he sees or foresees in them but only to the praise of his glory.

Returning to the thought that God's elect are a remnant, a small number, we should pause to commend the sensitive statement on this matter in the *Second Helvetic*, Chapter 10:

> Although God knows who are his, and here and there mention is made of the small number of the elect, yet we must hope well of all, and not rashly judge any man to be a reprobate. . . .
>
> And when the Lord was asked whether there were few that should be saved, he does not answer and tell them that few or many should be saved or damned, but rather he exhorts everyman to "strive to enter by the narrow door" (Lu. 13:24): as if he should say, It is not for you curiously to inquire about these matters.

Though we should not speculate about how many are elect and why they seem to be a minority, we might nonetheless learn something from a consideration of such questions. For instance, we might note that our stress on large numbers appears to be more of a pagan heresy than a biblical doctrine. Like the ancient Romans, Americans are especially prone to equate size with significance. Recalling that the

---

107. Spurgeon, *Lectures to My Students* (Grand Rapids: Zondervan, 1958), 2: 20.

church is the heir with Israel of God's electing grace and that God told Israel that he had chosen them "not because you were more in number than any other people" (Deut. 7:7) should help us restrain our penchant for impressive statistics. The doctrine of election reminds us that "God moves in a mysterious way, his wonders to perform." When E. F. Schumacher, a British economist, wrote a book entitled *Small Is Beautiful: Economics as If People Mattered*, he raised questions that have theological implications as well. Too often a commendable zeal for "church growth" betrays one into the tyranny of numbers, of equating worth with size. Though small may be beautiful, the assumption is too often that big is much more so.[108]

No one ever castigated "Christendom" more scathingly for its stress on numbers than Kierkegaard. In his *Attack on Christendom*, he accuses the state church of Denmark of having made the narrow gate that leads to life into the broad gate that leads to "Christendom." Thus, he complains, "we Danes seek to fool God with myriads of name Christians so that he will not perceive that there is not one true Christian in Denmark." According to Kierkegaard, the ideas of the state and of Christianity are mutually antithetical:

> Although the strength of the state is directly proportional to numbers in population, Christianity is vital with an inverse relation to numbers and its strength is dependent upon the intensity of devotion found in the few.[109]

This approach of Kierkegaard, which enabled him to say that "One single true Christian is enough to justify the assertion that Christianity exists," is in my opinion more reflective of the Bible than Barth's extended effort in the *Dogmatics* to number Judas among the elect. Why should we fear that the existence of one single human reprobate were enough to justify the denial that Christianity exists?[110]

---

108. For more on this, see the perceptive article by Peter Monkres, pastor of a small church in Colorado—"Small Is Beautiful: Churches as if People Mattered," *Christian Century*, 10 May 1978, pp. 492–93.

109. Kierkegaard, quoted in *Masterpieces of Christian Literature*, ed. F. N. Macgill (New York: Harper, 1963), p. 730.

110. See pp. 48–54 herein. By a true reprobate, I mean one who, unlike Barth's "Reprobate," Jesus Christ, never triumphs over death. Such a true reprobate is one who remains spiritually dead, choosing, like Milton's Satan, to reign in hell rather than serve in heaven.

Christianity is obviously the religion of the minority, both in terms of the statistics in the handbooks of world religions and in terms of the biblical theology of the Remnant. Grounding this minority status in the doctrine of election, however, has generally been resisted even by those who accept their remnant identity. They reject the implication that the majority of humankind is condemned in the divine purpose. Augustine's decision in favor of double predestination was aggravated by his conviction that salvation was indissolubly linked to the sacrament of baptism. This placed even infants who died unbaptized in the *limbus infantum*, beyond the pale of the beatific vision. Though the evangelical and Reformed Protestants repudiated the thought that unbaptized infants, dying in infancy, were condemned for want of the sacrament, they nonetheless hesitated in many instances to affirm that all infants dying in infancy are elect. In Michael Wigglesworth's celebrated poem "The Day of Doom" (1662), God reasons on the judgment day with reprobate infants, who "from the womb unto the tomb were straightway carried," about the justice of their doom. In the end, like Dante's Virgil and other noble heathen, they are assigned the most comfortable accommodations in hell.

In more recent times the doctrine of the universal salvation of infants dying in infancy has been generally espoused. In view of the high rate of infant mortality throughout the millennia of human history, this conclusion obviously did a great deal to swell the number of the elect! In the last sentence of the last volume of his *Systematic Theology*, Charles Hodge asserts that the number of the lost will in the end prove "very inconsiderable as compared with the whole number of the saved" (3: 880). One problem with such reasoning is that it seems to imply that while a small part of the elect attain salvation by a holy life, the large majority attain it by an untimely death. It is a teasing speculation to wonder whether the Grim Reaper might not have gained more souls for paradise than all the evangelists and missionaries together!

Others have followed the lead of Zwingli and reasoned that in the case of exceptional piety (the "noble heathen"), God's electing grace may extend not only to infants who die in infancy but also to adults who live beyond the pale of the church visible and the proclamation of the gospel. Speaking of the nations that have never had the advantage of hearing the word preached, Zanchius concludes that they must be strangers to the faith that comes thereby, and yet he adds that "It is not, indeed, improbable, but some individuals in these unenlightened countries might belong to the secret election of grace; and the habit of faith might be wrought in these."[111] Even the Westminster Confession speaks of God's saving "elect persons who are incapable of being outwardly called by the ministry of the Word" (chap. 10, sect. 3). While the authors were doubtless thinking of the mentally and emotionally incapacitated, there is no warrant from Scripture to limit the interpretation of the Confession to these unhappy creatures. Hence, even

---

111. Zanchius, *Absolute Predestination*, p. 104.

where one would not expect it, suggestions have been made that expand the circle of the elect.

Second Addendum: Election and Preaching

In the opinion of many, election and preaching are mutually exclusive. Those who think in this way conclude, as did Wesley, that were election true, preaching would be vain, for the elect will be saved anyway. A causal-deterministic view of election might well lead to such a conclusion.[112] William Carey, the father of modern missions, had to contend with the argument that in his own time God would save the heathen without our help. As a member of the Particular Baptist Association, and himself a Calvinist, Carey had reason to entitle his influential book on missions *An Enquiry into the Obligation of Christians to Use Means for the Conversion of the Heathen* (1792). In making the point that means must be used to convert the lost, Carey was simply reflecting what the New Testament teaches: "How are men to call upon him in whom they have not believed? And how are they to believe in him of whom they have not heard? And how are they to hear without a preacher? And how can men preach unless they are sent?" (Rom. 10:14–15). While it is "of his own will," as James reminds us, that God "brought us forth," yet it is also "by [means of] the word of truth" (James 1:18).

We do not intend, by quoting such Scripture on the importance of means, to remove all paradox from our discussion of the subject. Election makes preaching a paradox *in praxi* corresponding to the paradoxes *in thesi* we have already discussed. When Paul (in Corinth) is told by the Lord in a vision, "I have many people in this city" (Acts 18:10), he neither asks who they might be in the interest of efficiency nor departs for another city on the assumption that in that case they will be saved regardless of what he does. He rather stays a year and six months teaching God's word among them, no

---

112. Witness, for example, the Old School Baptists, sometimes called "Anti-effort" or "Anti-Mission" Baptists, who view mission societies, Sunday schools, and similar institutions as human contrivances that assume that salvation depends on human effort. These hyper-Calvinistic Baptists became prominent, especially in the South, in the mid-nineteenth century (see A. H. Newman's *History of the Baptist Churches in the United States* [New York: Scribners, 1918], pp. 433–42).

doubt with tears and with trials, going from house to house, as he did in Ephesus (Acts 20:19—20, 31).[113]

The paradox of which we speak confronts us in the New Testament frequently. "No one," says our Lord, "can come to me unless the Father who sent me draws him" (John 6:44). But he does not say, in his invitation to sinners, "Come unto me, all you who are drawn of my Father" (see Matt. 11:28.)[114] At another time he declares, "All that the Father gives me will come to me; and him who comes to me I will not cast out" (John 6:37). Calvinists like to quote the former half of this verse, and Arminians the latter half. But any attempt to bring the two parts of the verse together so as to attain a self-evident harmony would inevitably end in the creation of a different text. In order to exorcise the paradox of divine sovereignty (those given shall come) and human contingency (whoever comes may be assured of acceptance) from this word of our Lord, we would have to make it read either (1) I will not cast out any whom the Father has given me when they come to me, or (2) I will not cast out any who come to me, for my Father desires all to come. The long and the short of it is that when we apply such a rational method, we end up not with the Christian Bible but with the Deist's Bible of John Toland, which was appropriately named *Christianity Not Mysterious*.[115]

This paradox of theory and practice in Scripture accounts for what may be called "kerygmatic universality" on the one hand, and

---

113. This paradox of laboring diligently to accomplish a divine purpose already fixed in the mind of God has been given many "explanations." Max Weber, for example, argues that because the decree of election is secret, some people were driven to frenetic activity in order to assure their salvation, thus paradoxically becoming theoretical fatalists and psychological activists (see Berkouwer's discussion of Weber's position in *Divine Election*, pp. 280ff.). For those standing within the circle of faith, it is enough that we have been loved even though unlovely and thus, "constrained by that love," do what we do in gratitude to him who loved us (2 Cor. 5:14).

114. Witness the jejune observation of Amyraut: "No one speaks in this manner to invite us to faith: 'Believe, for God has ordained from all eternity whether or not you will' " (cited by Armstrong, *Calvinism and the Amyraut Heresy*, p. 167).

115. Toland proceeds in his subtitle to rule out any lingering doubt concerning his thesis: *A Treatise Showing That There Is Nothing in the Gospel Contrary to Reason, or above It: And That No Christian Doctrine Can Properly Be Called a Mystery*.

"didactic particularity" on the other.[116] In the New Testament, "kerygmatic universality" is illustrated in the Great Commission (Matt. 28:19) and in the preaching of the apostles. Jesus commands the apostles to preach to *all* nations, and according to Luke's sermon summaries in the book of Acts, the accent in the apostles' preaching was on the need of all who heard to repent and believe the gospel. Nevertheless, the way in which those converted as a result of this kerygmatic effort are regularly addressed in the epistles illustrates "didactic particularity." For example, Peter's characterization of his Christian readers in 1 Peter 1:1–2 literally means "the elect sojourners of the diaspora . . . predestined by God the Father" (εκλεκτοις παρεπιδημοις διασπορας, . . . κατα προγνωσιν θεου πατρος). How different from the address with which he began his sermon on the day of Pentecost (Acts 2:14): "Men of Judea, . . . let this be known to you, and give ear to my words" (Ανδρες Ιουδαιοι . . . τουτο υμιν γμωστον εστω και ενωτισασθε τα ρηματα μου). In Thessalonica Paul preached to all those gathered in the synagogue that Jesus was the Christ (Acts 17:3), but later, when he writes to his converts in that city (1 Thess. 1:4), he thanks God that "we know . . . that he has chosen you" (ειδοτες . . . την εκλογην υμων), thanks God that he had "not destined [τιθημι] us for wrath, but to obtain salvation" (1 Thess. 5:9). In summary, we could say that the apostles preached to their pagan hearers in terms of the book of Moses and the prophets, but spoke to their converts in terms of the Book of Life.

The distinction between the kerygmatic and the didactic that I have used to illumine the paradox of election and preaching—a nuance of the larger paradox of the divine and the human in salvation—is more easily applied to the preaching situation of the New Testament than to that of our own day for the simple reason that we tend not to draw such sharp lines between Christians and non-Christians. Ministers in contemporary pulpits find themselves expected to fill the roles both of evangelist and teacher. Their congregations tend to be made up of pagan saints and saintly pagans rather than of pagans *or* saints. Times, situations, and attitudes dictate different approaches to the question of how one should treat the subject of election in preaching.

---

116. The former phrase is Berkouwer's; I have coined the latter.

ELECTION AND THE INDIVIDUAL

In the Reformed and Puritan tradition, election has sometimes been overtly proclaimed even in an evangelistic situation. Jonathan Edwards registered amazement that those of his sermons that stressed the sovereignty of God and the unworthiness of sinners were the most effective in leading to conversion (see his *Faithful Narrative of the Surprising Work of God* [1737]). However, when John de St. Andre preached on predestination at the Friday convocation in St. Peters, Geneva, nearly two hundred years earlier (on 16 Oct. 1551), Bolsec interrupted the sermon to denounce the godless notion that the Almighty decides the fate of people before they are born. For his effort Bolsec was arrested by the police and charged with disturbing the peace.

Probably no one ever preached the doctrine of election more overtly (and eloquently) to more people over a longer period of time than C. H. Spurgeon. In our day, on the other hand, the subject is often passed over even in Reformed pulpits—a fact that has led James Daane to comment, "When the sound of election is no longer heard in the pulpits of churches creedally committed to the truth of election, the situation would appear to warrant an investigation to discover whether the pulpit or the doctrine is at fault."[117] Daane feels the fault is not with the pulpit but with the doctrine as defined by Dort and proceeds to redefine it in his own distinctive way.

A final word of caution is in order. Helpful as the distinction between the kerygmatic and didactic may be, we ought not to press it overly much when reflecting on the paradox of election and preaching, since we are speaking of distinction only, not of separation. Preaching involves teaching; and teaching—of the truths of the Christian faith, in any case—involves preaching. Were we to separate the teaching ministry of the church from its preaching ministry, we would run the risk, especially with the doctrine of election, of building a wall between the church and the world. While the church as the elect people of God is called out of the sinful world (2 Cor. 6:17), the church can never completely separate itself from the world as God will separate the wheat from the tares in the judgment day. The church and the world are not "we" and "they" in this radical, eschatological sense. As yet no great chasm has been

---

117. Daane, *The Freedom of God: A Study in Election and Pulpit* (Grand Rapids: William B. Eerdmans, 1973), p. 6.

fixed that one should not pass over to the other (Luke 16:26). The church is called to speak to the world, not to speculate about its destiny. Preaching, in other words, is of the essence and definition of the church. Where the gospel is not preached—that is, heralded to the lost world—the church does not exist in the New Testament sense.

Furthermore, a faulty understanding of election threatens not only the existential nature of faith but the existential nature of preaching as well. While few would go as far as Wesley did in the heat of controversy and charge those who hold to the doctrine of election with making preaching vain, it is the case that those in the Calvinistic tradition often consider preaching to be a mere instrument by which God's electing purpose is fulfilled. While there are surely worse theologies of preaching, we must nonetheless charge this view with falling short of the New Testament view of the matter on the grounds that it does not adequately account for the intensity evidenced by the apostles in carrying out their mission, for the sense of "necessity" they felt had been "laid upon them," or for the sacrifice and tears of a David Brainerd, a John Eliot, or a William Carey—Calvinists all and preachers *par excellence*.

It is preaching, preaching in the New Testament sense, that mediates eternal election in the temporal moment of calling. Berkouwer states that the way Bavinck relates preaching to election and what he has to say about election is in his opinion "the profoundest part of his dogmatics. The gate to the *kerygma* is thrown wide open, not inspite of, but because of the freedom of election, which is not the freedom of a *dominum absolutum* or *potentia absoluta*, but of the living God of salvation."[118] That is to say, preaching is ultimately an act of the electing God. As the ambassador of Christ, the preacher is the human instrument through whom God makes his appeal to the sinner. In a profound sense, Christ validates himself in preaching. He is not simply the object of preaching but its Subject. And when Christ is so preached that he is himself the ultimate Preacher, then regardless of whether one happens to be preaching about election, one will be preaching in terms of election.

---

118. Berkouwer, *Divine Election*, p. 225.

CONCERNING WONDER AND WORSHIP

We have ruminated on the mystery with which the doctrine of divine predestination confronts us and the inability of theologians to overcome the paradoxes in which that mystery is expressed. This Augustinian sense of mystery and the wonder it evokes pertains, as we have noted, not only to those who are accepted, but especially to those who are rejected. The efforts of scholars to cast the light of rational understanding on the issue of reprobation have been less than satisfying, to say the least. Laypersons consulting some contemporary version of the New Testament may feel relieved to read "Jacob have I loved, but Esau have I loved less" or "I have preferred Jacob to Esau," but these efforts of translators-turned-exegetes to soften the original amount to little more than word games. The text (Rom. 9:13) simply says, "Jacob have I loved, but Esau have I hated" (Τον Ιακωβ ηγαπησα, τον δε Ησαυ εμισησα).[119] Nor is it especially helpful to point out that in the original context (Mal. 1:2–3) reference is being made to the descendants of Jacob and Esau—the nations of Israel and Edom—rather than to the brothers as such. Here, as throughout Rom. 9–11, the national and the individual strands of the argument are so intertwined that they cannot be separated along theological party lines. Obviously, the apostle is thinking of individuals as well as nations, since in the previous verse (9:12) he quotes the oracle to Rebecca before she gave birth to her sons (Gen. 25:23). And the remark that he makes in the verse previous to that (9:11) is as forthright as it is awesome: he states that this oracle was pronounced not only before the children were born but before they had done good or evil, in order that (ινα of purpose) the electing purpose of God might stand. This, I would submit, should be enough to stop any theological speculation in its tracks. As Alford reminds us, "It is in parts of Scripture like this that we must be especially careful not to fall short of what is written, nor

---

[119]. Of course translators are not the only ones to succumb to such efforts. Harry Boer comments on the relation of semantics to theology when he observes that Dort repudiates the thought that God condemns the reprobate "by a mere arbitrary act of his will" but affirms that he did so "according to his sovereign good pleasure" (*The Doctrine of Reprobation* [Grand Rapids: William B. Eerdmans, 1983], pp. 41–42). It would seem that the line between indignation and reverence can be nicely drawn.

to allow of any compromise of the plain and awful words of God's Spirit for the sake of a caution which he himself does not teach us."[120]

And what shall we say to the argument that in the day of judgment the sheep only, not the goats, are the object of an eternal decree (Matt. 25:31–46)?[121] It is true, of course, that the eternal fire to which the latter depart is not said to be prepared for them "from the foundation of the world," as is the kingdom that the righteous inherit. But when we read that it was prepared for the devil and his angels, the argument seems to afford slight comfort. Nor is there anything substantially convincing about the argument that unbelievers who stumble at Christ are altogether the agents of their own undoing (1 Pet. 2:8). The phrase οι προσκοπτουσιν τω λογω απειθουντες εις ο και ετεθησαν does not mean "Because they were disobedient to the word, they were destined to stumble." Rather, both their stumbling and their disobedience are embraced somehow—who can say how?—in a larger purpose that has assigned all (τιθημι) a place.

Rather than probe the question of the reprobate, rather than seek to "explain" the texts which speak of their end, we would do well to heed the example of Scripture, which teaches us to worship him whose awesome severity is just, even as his mercy is everlasting. The Song of Moses—which is in heaven's hymnbook (Rev. 15:3–4)—is occasioned by the judgment of the Egyptians as well as by the deliverance of the Israelites (Exod. 14–15). Well might God's people burst forth in songs of gratitude at the Red Sea, for they know themselves to be the beneficiaries of his great deliverance. But their worship is foiled by the note of judgment reiterated—like the theme of Ravel's *Bolero*—in plague after plague on Egypt, culminating at last as the waters overwhelm the Egyptian hosts, the purpose for which God raised Pharaoh up (Rom. 9:17). It is as this dark purpose is fulfilled that his saving purpose is also fulfilled. But why this should be is his secret.

Our hymnals may no longer contain Watts's reminder that

He struck the sons of Egypt dead;

---

120. H. Alford, *The Greek Testament*, 4 vols., 7th ed. (Cambridge: Deighton, Bell and Co., 1875), 4: 409.
121. Cf. Brunner, *Dogmatics*, 1: 326ff.

> How mighty is his rod!
> And thence with joy his people led:
> How gracious is our God!

but our Bibles still contain Psalm 136, from which he drew his inspiration. And the Spirit, who inspired the original psalmist, taught him — and us — to respond not only to the deliverance of Israel but also to the overthrow of Pharaoh's hosts with the same antiphonal: "for his steadfast love endures for ever." How, then, can we dismiss this ancient song from the psalter as of no account? Are we not as Christians the heirs with Israel of the same election and salvation? That is why the concluding book of the New Testament joins the Song of Moses with that of the Lamb: they are not two songs but one, for God's covenant is one, even as he is one. And it is to this one God that the beatified saints sing, even as they contemplate the angels with the seven last plagues:

> Great and wonderful are thy deeds,
> O Lord God the Almighty!
> Just and true are thy ways,
> O King of the ages! (Rev. 15:3)

Here we do well to remember Deuteronomy 29:29, which reminds us (especially the theologians) that there are secret things that belong to the Lord. But this same text, as we have already noted, also speaks of things revealed — and surely predestination, for all its hiddenness, is a truth revealed. It is this that allows us to venture to investigate the paradoxes that the doctrine poses for all who reflect upon it.

Yet after all our investigation, the mystery remains, for the revealed things are like the tip of an iceberg: their disclosure only opens up larger mysteries.[122] As revealed, the doctrine of election serves to assure us that we need not strive to attain our salvation by works; it is in fact the cornerstone of the doctrine of grace. As hidden, the doctrine conveys the awesome truth that not all are alike embraced in the divine favor. While some are elected, others are rejected; while some confess that the lines have fallen to them in pleasant places (Ps. 16:6), others stand outside the favored circle.

---

122. We ought not, in other words, to construe the "hidden things" the Deuteronomist ascribes to God and the "revealed things" that belong to us as mutually exclusive categories.

ELECTION AND PREDESTINATION

And even those who stand within cannot discover the reason why. Here also there is mystery. Israel is not loved (nor is the church) because of its great numbers, nor because of anything else, but only because the Lord loved his chosen (Deut. 7:6–8). Election, then, is a truth that we grasp existentially—or, we might say, a truth that grasps us. And as those who are grasped by this truth, we cannot doubt that we are chosen in Christ. This is the truth in and by which we live as Christians.

Apropos of this existential character of our election and the contemporary emphasis on theology as story, it is interesting to note that in the book of Acts, Luke includes the story of Paul's conversion on the Damascus road three times over (Acts 9:1–19; 22:3–16; 26:12–23). And it is, indeed, some story. On the lips of the apostle himself, it tells us in a more gripping and effective way what election means than any dogmatic treatise ever could.

> "Brothers and fathers, hear the defense which I now make before you."
>
> And when they heard that he addressed them in the Hebrew language, they were the more quiet. And he said: "I am a Jew, born in Tarsus in Cilicia, but brought up in this city at the feet of Gamaliel, educated according to the strict manner of the law of our fathers, being zealous for God as you are this day. I persecuted this Way to the death, binding and delivering to prison both men and women, as the high priest and the whole council of elders bear me witness. From them I received letters to the brethren, and I journeyed to Damascus to take those also who were there and bring them in bonds to Jerusalem to be punished.
>
> "As I made my journey and drew near to Damascus, about noon a great light shone about me. And I fell to the ground and heard a voice saying to me 'Saul, Saul, why do you persecute me?' And I answered, 'Who are you, Lord?' And he said to me, 'I am Jesus of Nazareth, whom you are persecuting.' Now those who were with me saw the light but did not hear the voice of the one speaking to me. And I said, 'What shall I do, Lord?' And the Lord said to me, 'Rise, and go into Damascus, and there you will be told all that is appointed [τετακται, 'ordained,' 'ordered'] for you to do.' " (Acts 22:1–10)

Commenting years later on this experience, Paul writes, "But when he who had set me apart before I was born, and had called me through his grace, was pleased to reveal his Son to me, in order that I might preach him among the Gentiles, I did not confer with flesh and blood. . . but I went away into Arabia" (Gal. 1:15–17). No wonder Paul was Mr. Election! And when one reads the conversion story of St. Augustine, one understands why the Bishop of Hippo understood the apostle to the Gentiles so well. Though the setting of one story is the road to Damascus and the other a garden in Milan, it is in the last analysis the same story, the story of God's sovereign grace.

But when we press the implications—when we seek a congruent, rational explanation of why God elects some, of why he appeared to a Paul and not to a Caiaphas—we are reminded that God's "judgments are unsearchable, and his ways past finding out." Indeed, when the apostle Paul reflected on these matters, he found himself caught up in the very paradox revealed in the life of our Lord, a paradox of which we have already spoken. As Jesus wept over Jerusalem (Luke 19:41), so Paul sorrowed over his people and could wish himself accursed from Christ for their sakes (Rom. 9:3). Yet as Jesus exulted in the Spirit and thanked his Father, who had hidden the truth from the wise and understanding (Luke 10:21), so Paul also breaks forth into praise as he contemplates the "depth of the riches and wisdom and knowledge of God" (Rom. 11:33).

This paradox of sorrow and praise reflects, as we have already intimated, the ultimate paradox at the heart of the doctrine of grace: the veiled character of revelation. God remains hidden even in his revelation, for he is the Transcendent One whose thoughts are higher than ours, the Holy One whose ways are past finding out. Yet at the same time he is Love, that "Love Divine, all loves excelling, Joy of heaven, to earth come down." Hence, as scientists have their doctrine of the incomprehensibility of the universe, so theologians have their doctrine of the incomprehensibility of the God who made the universe. It is this mystery of the divine nature that in the final analysis explains why the two rationally satisfying positions on predestination—supralapsarianism and restitutionism—are both untenable. The former impugns the love of God; the latter impugns his holiness.[123]

The doxology at the end of Romans 11, in which Paul ascribes

---

123. By the same token, it was Barth's attempt to combine these two that doomed his effort to failure.

glory to the God from whom and through whom and to whom are all things, falls at the end of the most searching discussion of the subject of election in the New Testament. Such a location is appropriate, inasmuch as doxology, the language of worship, is the only language ultimately commensurate to the subject. As Weber has observed,

> The "mystery" of which Paul speaks (Rom. 11:25) is not susceptible of dogmatic interpretation. It is striking that where such final visions occur the New Testament completely abandons speech from which conceptual inferences can be drawn and uses speech which merges with the tone of a hymn of meditation—as happens in Rom. 11:32f.[124]

While the position of Rudolf Otto on predestination is in certain ways different from ours, there are some significant affinities. What we have expressed in terms of Kierkegaardian *existenz* he describes in the language of the mystic. Though he does not regard the Christianity of Paul (and John) as mysticism, he does think that it is "religion tinged with mysticism."[125] He suggests that the paradoxes of the Trinity and Christology can, with the help of interpretation, be tolerated even by the rationalist, but he astutely observes that predestination—especially in its Pauline and Johannine form—has always been the rock of offense above all others. (He allows that this is not true of Schleiermacher's restatement of the doctrine, in which the offense is simply removed.)

Otto distinguishes rather sharply between election and predestination. Election, he maintains, has to do with the sinner's awareness of salvation as a gift; it urges upon sinners an awareness of themselves as passive recipients of divine grace. But he holds that predestination to life and to death (what he calls *predestinatio ambigua* because it is dark, obscure, and unpredictable) is quite another matter. While both election and predestination have to do with the *numinosen*, he says, in the latter the awareness of the *mysterium tremendum* is expressed in the creature's feelings of "becoming nothing" over against the Transcendent Majesty. One's own powers, claims, and significance are of no consequence in the presence of the Transcendent; one becomes nothing in one's willing and running, one's being and deciding. On the creaturely side, then, there is only weakness; on the numinal side, there is almightiness. On the creaturely side, there is only the demise of all self-determination; on the side of the Numinous, there is all-determining and disposing power.[126]

---

124. Weber, *Grundlagen der Dogmatik*, 2: 545. Here Weber perceptively notes that "It is striking that R. Bultmann, in his *Theologie des Neuen Testament*, 1953, which is supposed to be completely historical, utters not a word about Rom. 9–11." Indeed!

125. Otto, *Das Heilige* (Munich: C. H. Becksche, 1936), p. 106n.1.

126. See Otto, *Das Heilige*, pp. 106–8.

ELECTION AND THE INDIVIDUAL

It was Augustine, designated by the church the "doctor of grace," who first emphasized the *mystery* of that grace. As Jaroslav Pelikan has suggested, for Augustine "it was ultimately an unfathomable mystery why one should receive grace and another should not receive it, when neither of them deserved to receive it. The words of Romans 11:33 were his constant reply to those who wanted the mystery resolved."[127] Only as we view the divine goodness and severity in this way does the "mystery of godliness" awaken in us the wonder, the awe, the worship to which Augustine, emulating Paul, calls us. On this point even Calvin cites Augustine at some length:

> You, a man, expect an answer from me; I too am a man. Therefore, let both of us hear one who says, "O man, who are you?" Ignorance that believes is better than rash knowledge. . . . "O depth!" Thou seekest a reason? I tremble at the depth. Reason, thou; I will marvel. Dispute, thou; I will believe. I see the depth; I do not reach the bottom. Paul rested, for he found wonder. He calls God's judgments "unsearchable," and thou seekest out to search them? He speaks of his ways as "inscrutable," and thou dost track them down? (*Inst.*, 3, 23, 5)

This language of awe, this note of worship struck by Augustine, reminds us that the matrix of all theology is the worshiping congregation, for it was out of the experience of worship that theology was born. Election, like all other doctrines, must be understood from this perspective. The voluminous treatments in dogmatic treatises can provide only a secondary, not a primary, word on the subject. The primary word is the "Amen" with which the elect community ascribes eternal glory and dominion "to him who loves us and who has freed us from our sins by his blood and who has made us a kingdom, priests to his God and Father" (Rev. 1:5–6). Salvation is his work, not ours; it is of grace—all of grace. This is the truth we confess in the doctrine of election and the truth that we seal with a solemn Amen.

---

127. Pelikan, *The Christian Tradition*, 1: 298.

Index of Names and Subjects

Alcuin, 7
Alford, Henry, 105, 133-34
Amyrauldism: summarized, 101-2
Amyraut, Moise, 86, 101-2, 129n.114
Angels: fallen are replaced by the elect, 121n.99
Anselm, 9, 122n.99
Anti-effort Baptists, 128n.112
Anti-Semitism, 35, 37
Apokatastasis. *See* Universalism
Aquinas, Thomas, 9n.6, 19, 98, 99n.70, 122; on predestination, 9, 10; on relation between election and providence, 22
Aquitanus, Prosper, 7
Arminianism, 14-15, 17, 72-73
Arminius, Jacobus, 14, 14n.12, 14n.13, 15, 69, 77, 92; heretical views of, 15n.14; interpretation of Romans 9, 72; predestination based on foreknowledge, 69, 72-73; repudiation of election, 63
Assurance of election, 57-60
Athanasius, 5n.1
Augustine, 1, 1n.1, 3, 6n.2, 6n.4, 7, 9, 12, 16, 17, 19, 28, 54, 58, 62, 68n.29, 71, 74, 78, 97, 121, 121n.98, 127, 237; on election viewed as double predestination, 5, 6; on election related to soteriology, 22; and the mystery of grace, 139; understanding of Matthew 22:14, 99, 123, 123n.103
Baillie, John, 124
Barclay, William, 71n.34, 76n.39, 80

Barth, Karl, 3, 19n.17, 20, 55n.8, 58, 60n.18, 62, 65, 68n.29, 92n.55, 99n.70, 107, 110n.84, 121n.98, 126; and decretal theology, 23; failure of his position, 137n.123; infralapsarianism rejected, 85-86; supralapsarianism defended, 89-90; view of election summarized, 19, 48-54
Bavinck, Herman, 98, 132
Bede, 7
Berkouwer, G. C., 19n.17, 59n.14, 91, 109, 125, 132
Beza, Theodore, 12, 14n.12, 63, 65, 101; and decretal theology, 22, 64
Black, James M., 105n.76
Boer, Harry, 62, 94n.56, 133n.119
Bolsec, Jerome, 63, 131
Bonaventura, 9
Book of Life, 59, 60
Bruce, F. F., 122n.100
Brunner, Emil, 19, 20-21, 51-52, 99, 111, 123n.103
Bucer, Martin, 10
Bullinger, Heinrich, 63, 91, 112n.88
Bultmann, Rudolph, 138n.124
Bunyan, John, 60n.17, 95n.62
Caesarius of Arles, 7
Calvin, John, 1n.1, 10, 11n.9, 14n.12, 15n.14, 17, 19, 50, 58, 64, 68n.29, 79-83, 92, 139; on Christ the mirror of election, 56; as double predestinarian, 12, 14; and the locus of election, 22; and the Jews, 36; prolonged defense of election, 62-63; "will of God" used in double sense, 100-101

INDEX OF NAMES AND SUBJECTS

Canons of Dort, 58, 85 n.49, 91 n.54, 93, 94 n.56
Carey, William, 128, 132
Castellio, Sebastian, 82 n.47
Chafer, Louis S., 45
Chrysostom, John, 71, 71 n.34
Church: heir of Israel's election, 33; mutuality in Israel's and Gentiles' salvation, 41; its relation to Israel, 31-33; supplants Israel, 36-37
Church of England: election in the Anglo-Catholic tradition, 73 n.36; view of election, 15, 16, 59
Clement XI, 11 n.8
Cowper, William, 123
Daane, James, 131
Decretal theology, 22-23, 64; given confessional status, 65; modified in Westminster Confession, 75 n.38
Deism, 129
Dispensationalism, 45-46
Determinism, 111, 112 n.88
Dodd, C. H., 80
Donne, John, 57
Eastern Orthodox Church: interpretation of Romans 9, 71-72; view of election, 68-69
Edwards, Jonathan, 16, 131
Elect as a fixed number, 6, 10, 13; Augustine's affirmation, 121-28; Barth's rejection, 20, 50, 121 n.98; Kierkegaard's view, 126; smallness of number, 122-24
Election: and assurance, 57-60; based on foreknowledge, 14, 15, 66, 68-73; comfort of, 59-60; corporate and individual, 48; illustrated in the story of Paul's conversion, 136-37; and Jesus Christ, 54-56; its location in systematics, 22, 64-67; meaning of, 3-4; teleological approach, 31 n.1; understood cosmically, 118-20; understood existentially, 136; understood *sub specie aeternitatis*, 3, 64, 83; understood *sub specie temporis*, 2, 61-68, 102
Eternity related to time as election to calling, 109
Fall: in Amyraut's thought, 86; in infralapsarianism, 85, 95-96; a mystery, 92; and the purpose of God, 84; in supralapsarianism, 88-89
Foreknowledge: as basis of election, 68-73; the meaning of "fore," 109, 111, 113
Free will: in Arminius's thought, 69; in the Eastern Church, 68 n.30; and election, 73-76; paradoxically related to the divine freedom, 76, 76 n.39; and predestination, 9
Gibbon, Edward, 103
God: not the author of sin, 91-92, 94; incomprehensibility of, 137. *See also* Will of God
Gomarus, Francis, 14 n.12, 15
Gospel: offered to all, 28, 29, 106 n.77
Gottschalk, 7, 7 n.5, 8, 64, 78
Greek Fathers' view of election, 68-69
Heppe, Heinrich Ludwig, 65
Herder, Johann Gottfried von, 61-62
Hincmar, 7 n.5
Hodge, Charles, 127; and the future of the Jews, 43-44
Horrible decree, 82
How, William Walsham, 119
Infants and election, 127
Infralapsarianism: and the purpose of God, 84, 85, 87; in the Reformed tradition, 89, 93, 94; Zanchius's exposition and defense, 94-96
Innocent X, 11
Isidore of Seville, 7
Israel and election, 30-31
Jansen, Cornelius, 10-11
Jansenism, 10-11
Jeremias, Joachim, 119 n.93
Jews: and the church, 34; the first Christians, 33; their future, 34-39, 43
John of Damascus, 98
John XXIII, 37
Judas: Barth's view of, 53-54
Justin Martyr, 5
Kierkegaard, Søren, 126
Leo XIII, 9 n.6
Liberalism and election, 17
Lindsey, Hal, 45
Logic: acknowledged by Berkouwer, 109; its limitations, 106, 108
Louis XIV, 11 n.8
Lutheranism, 11-12, 73 n.36
Luther, Martin, 9 n.6, 10, 11, 12 n.10, 15 n.14, 17, 89, 110; attitude toward the Jews, 35-36; view of Christ's election, 56
Maccovius, 92

INDEX OF NAMES AND SUBJECTS

Maurus, Rabanus, 7
Melanchthon, Philipp, 10, 11, 11 n.9
Methodism: view of election, 16
Muller, Richard, 23 n.18
Mystery of election, 6, 12, 14, 28, 133-39

Ness, Christopher, 63-64

Origen, 51, 71, 71 n.34, 115 n.90
Original sin: Augustinian view, 74
Orthodox Church. *See* Eastern Orthodox Church
Otto, Rudolph, 138
Owen, John, 81 n.44

Paradox: basis of both joy and sorrow, 137; of grace, 7, 106-9; nature of, 108; necessity of, 114-15; of sovereign purpose and the use of means, 128-29
Pascal, Blaise, 11
Paul: his conversion story, 136-37; his hopes for Israel, 38-44
Pelagius, 1, 6, 7; view of election, 5, 6 n.2
Pelikan, Jaraslav, 139
Perronet, Edward, 31
Pighius, Albert, 63, 100
Preaching: and election, 27-29, 128-32; includes teaching, 131
Predestination: Augustine's doctrine of, 93; Barth's view of, 20, 50-51; double, 6, 14; elaborated, 77-83; meaning and mystery of, 135, the meaning of the "pre," 109, 111, 113; Reformers' acceptance of, 10; Schleiermacher's rejection of, 18, 138; understood generally, 64

Remnant, 32-33; and the Second Helvetic Confession, 125
Reprobation, 26, 27, 97, 133, 134; in Augustine, 6 n.4; in Calvin, 79-83
Restitutionism, 20, 115 n.90, 116, 118
Ridderbos, Herman N., 41
Rowley, H. H., 3 n.2, 31 n.1
Ryrie, C. C., 45
Sayers, Dorothy, 47
Schlatter, A., 60, 107

Schleiermacher, Friedrich, 3 n.3, 17-19, 115, 115 n.90, 138
Schumacher, E. F., 126
Semi-Pelagianism, 7
Spurgeon, Charles, 64, 125, 131
Stone, Samuel J., 118
Supralapsarianism, 83-94; ethical problems of, 90-91, 93; and the logical order of thought, 86-87; rejected by the majority of Calvinists, 89-90
Syllogismus practicus, 57-60

Toland, John, 129
Toplady, Augustus, 96 n.63, 124 n.105; conflict with Wesley, 16 n.15
Toynbee, Arnold, 124
Trent, 10
TULIP, 15
Turretin, Francis, 94 n.57

Universalism, 20, 68 n.29; in Barth, 51-52, 92 n.55; kerygmatic universality and didactic particularity, 129-30; in relation to particularism, 115, 117-20; universalistic passages of Scripture, 103-5

Watson, Richard, 67
Watts, Isaac, 23, 80, 82 n.46, 118 n.92, 120, 124 n.104, 134-35
Weber, Max, 129 n.113
Weber, Otto, 62 n.21, 109; on the language of worship, 138
Wesley, Charles, 16 n.15, 75
Wesley, John, 59 n.15; on election, 16-17, 16 n.15; on election making preaching vain, 111 n.86, 128, 132
Whitefield, George, 16-17
Wigglesworth, Michael, 127
Will of God: as antecedent and consequent, 97-101, 107; as precept and purpose, 99-100; as secret and revealed, 99; as understood by Calvin, 81-82; both universal and particular, 28-29

Zanchius, Jerome, 16 n.15, 94-96, 122 n.101, 127
Zwingli, Ulrich, 10, 12, 64, 110, 127

Index of Scripture References

OLD TESTAMENT

Genesis
12:3   117
17:5   117
18:25   108
22:17   117
22:18   31, 41
25:23   133
26:4   31

Exodus
3:14   91, 108
4:19   81 n. 45
14–15   134
20:15   99

Numbers
33:9   30

Deuteronomy
7:1-5   31
7:6   30, 121
7:6-8   136
7:7   126
14:2   30
29:29   107, 135

Joshua
24:2   41
24:15   76

1 Samuel
10:24   54

1 Kings
19:18   122

Psalms
2:1   74
2:1-6   106
3:8   66
16:6   134
33:12   24
65:4   93
100:3   73
136   135

Isaiah
6:9-10   81 n. 45
6:9-13   32
6:10   27, 27 n. 3
7:3   32
8:2   32
8:18   32
9:12   32
14:24   87
29:10   28
41:8-10   30
42:1   54
43:10   31
46:10   84
49:6   31
55:6   116
55:8   106
65:2   70, 106

Jeremiah
18:4-5   80

Ezekiel
18:23   100

INDEX OF SCRIPTURE REFERENCES

33:11   70, 91, 106
40–48   46

Hosea
1:6-11   40

Amos
3:2   121, 125

9:7   40

Jonah
3:10–4:1   31

Malachai
1:2-3   133

NEW TESTAMENT

Matthew
3:5   104
3:7   104
6:10   100
7:13-14   123 n.102
8:11   118
11:25-27   27
11:28   129
12:18   54
13:13   27 n.2
16:16   34
21:43   32
22:14   99, 123
23:29ff.   40 n.10
23:37   106
23:41   96 n.64
24:22   24
25:31-45   134
25:31-46   116
25:41   90
26:39   106
28:19   117, 130
28:19-20   70

Mark
4:10-13   82 n.45
4:11   27
4:12   27
13:22   24
13:27   24
14:21   53
16:15   115

Luke
3:10ff.   104
8:9-10   27 n.2
9:35   47 n.1, 54
10:20   59
10:21   27, 106, 137
12:32   123
13:23   123
13:24   123, 125

14:28ff.   85
16:26   132
18:7   24
19:41   106, 137
23:35   47 n.1

John
1:3   51
1:29   29
3:16   29, 52, 106, 106 n.77, 115
3:18   52, 112
6:37   129
6:39   105
6:44   129
6:67-68   76
10:14   48
10:26   27
12:32   104
12:39   27, 27 n.3
15:16   48 n.4
15:19   48 n.4
17:2   25, 55
17:6   25, 55
17:9   25, 106
17:24   25, 55

Acts
1:24   26
1:26   26
2:5   103
2:14   130
2:23-26   53
3:21   118
4:25-28   106
6:5   26
9:1-19   136
9:6   100
10:1–11:18   34
10:34   125
11:18   28
13:46   41 n.11
13:48   26, 41 n.11, 122 n.100

INDEX OF SCRIPTURE REFERENCES

15:14   25
15:18   6
16:31   28, 112
17:3   130
17:26   26
17:28   74
17:30   28
18:10   25, 128
20:19-20   129
20:21   112, 116
21:31   129
22:1-10   136
22:3-16   136
26:12-23   136

Romans
1:16   41n.11
2:11   125
4:13   117
4:17   117
5:8   70
5:18   119, 119n.93
5:18-19   29
6:23   93, 118n.92
8:1   55
8:16   59
8:28   84, 116n.91
8:28-30   113
8:29   26, 39n.8, 59, 70, 109
8:30   56n.9
8:33   24
9–11   35-39, 40n.10, 48n.5, 76n.39, 133, 138n.124
9   61n.19, 71, 71n.34, 72
9:3   137
9:4-5   37
9:6-13 33
9:10-13   79
9:11   26, 71, 80, 133
9:11ff.   87
9:12   133
9:13   95n.61, 133
9:14-19   71
9:17   95n.61, 134
9:18   8, 27, 29n.5, 97, 105
9:19   71
9:20   14
9:20-21   72
9:20ff.   71
9:21ff.   80
9:22   106
9:22-23   116
9:22ff.   81
10:2   39
10:2-4 40
10:13   110
10:14-15   128
10:21   70, 106
11:1-2 35
11:2   39
11:2-7 40
11:4   122
11:7-8 27
11:8   28
11:11   41
11:12   42
11:15   41, 42
11:17-18   35
11:25   35, 36, 43, 121, 138
11:25-26   42
11:25ff.   35
11:26   35, 36
11:28   41
11:29   39
11:30-32   42
11:32-33   138
11:33   6, 43, 106, 137, 139

1 Corinthians
1:2   55
1:27-28   25
15:22   20, 55, 119

2 Corinthians
2:14-16   28
3:14-16   40
5:14   129n.113
5:14-15   70
5:19   29, 50
5:21   51
6:17   131
11:22   33

Galatians
1:15-17   137
2:20   48
3:8   117
3:17   39
3:28   24, 103
4:25   39
6:16   33

Ephesians
1:3-4   51
1:4   14, 49, 51, 57, 73, 109

INDEX OF SCRIPTURE REFERENCES

1:4-5   26, 33
1:9   120
1:10   120
1:11   26
1:20-23   120
2:8-9   112 n.87
2:13-15   120
2:14   118
3:8-12   88
3:10   33

Philippians
1:6   60
2:13   74
3:14   55
4:4   60

Colossians
1:23   103
3:11   106 n.77
3:12   25

1 Thessalonians
1:2-4   25
1:4   130
2:14-16   37, 40
2:16   40 n.10
5:9   130

2 Thessalonians
1:6-10   116
2:13   25

1 Timothy
2:4   29, 68, 70, 97, 98, 104, 105
2:5   51
2:5-6   29
5:21   55 n.8

2 Timothy
1:9   26, 109, 111 n.85
2:10   25
2:13   108

Titus
1:1   25
2:11   29
2:13   116

James
1:18   128
2:5   25

1 Peter
1:1-2   109, 130
1:2   70
1:17   125
2:4ff.   55
2:6-8   27, 116
2:8   134
2:9   33
2:9-10   125

2 Peter
1:10   32, 60
3:9   8, 29, 29 n.5, 104, 105

1 John
2:2   29, 115
3:14   60
3:24   59
4:16   91
4:19   107

2 John
13   47 n.1

Jude
3-4   27

Revelation
1:5-6   139
2:17   48
5:9   104, 119
6:11   121
6:16   116
7:9   123
13:8   54
14:6   119
15:3   135
15:3-4   134
17:14   25
19:1-8   88
20:6   90
20:7-10   123
20:14   90
21:1–22:5   90
21:3   90
21:5   90, 118
21:8   90
21:27   118
22:15   118
22:17   75 n.37
22:20   116